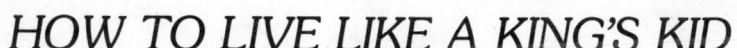

HOW TO LIVE LIKE A KING'S KID

HOW TO LIVE LIKE A KING'S KID

by Harold Hill

as told to

Irene Burk Harrell

Logos, International

Plainfield, New Jersey

Library of Congress Catalog Card Number: 73-93002

International Standard Book Number:
0-88270-083-9   (paper)
0-88270-086-3 (cloth)

Dedicated in grateful acknowledgment to:

my wife Ruth whom God used to get me to AA;

Alcoholics Anonymous, for introducing me to God;

my pastor, Peter Vroom, faithful shepherd,

to whom trouble is high adventure in Jesus

Contents

Contents (continued)

Preface

"Lord, do You really intend for Your people to live in a state of continuous victory in the midst of adversity?" That was the question I asked God just about twenty years ago, right after I met Jesus Christ as my Savior, Baptizer, and Healer.

His reply throughout the pages of the Manufacturer's Handbook, the Holy Bible, is an emphatic yes.

"Then how come so few live in victory?" I asked Him.

His answer came with clarity through such Scriptures as: I Corinthians 2:14: "The natural man receiveth not the things of the Spirit of God: for they are foolishness unto him;" Isaiah 1:5: "The whole head is sick;" and Colossians 2:8: "Beware lest any man spoil you through philosophy," which means, "Beware of philosophers, scoffers, whatiffers?, don't-you-supposers?, how-about-the-heatheners?, murmurers, and especially those drab, dreary dispensationalists who by devious evasions and cop-outs attempt to dispense with the miracles of God for today."

These Scriptures spoke loud and clear, and I knew the Number One hindrance to victorious living is the "Paralysis of Analysis" caused by the sick computer riding astride our shoulders, the rational commonsense mind, the Educated Idiot Box.

Even as God speaks in words of highest wisdom, *Come unto Me and find rest for your souls*, the EIB says, "No way—I'll do my own thing if it kills me." And it will.

God says, *Praise Me in the midst of trouble for guaranteed deliverance*. The EIB says, "Not until I see a change," and misses the blessing.

God says, *Let everything that hath breath praise Me.* The EIB says, "Wait until I catch my breath," and never does.

God says, *Read my Word, do it, and report on the results.* The EIB says, "But what about this? What if that? Suppose so and so?" and is a hearer only, and not a doer. The EIB makes of us the split-heads of James 1:8, double-minded men, and snatches defeat from certain victory.

God says, *Except ye become as a little child—* and the EIB scoffs, "Oversimplification!"

God says, *Prove me now,* and the EIB stalls, "Let me figure it out first and see if it fits into my theology."

This EIB principle stands out in Acts 4:13 where after seeing the disciples ministering charismatically with signs following, the Educated Idiots of the religious world were bugged because no one among the King's kids had a PhD.

And so, even now, as you read chapter one of this book, you might even detect the tendency in yourself to ask, "Why didn't the BOAC pilot fly out to sea and dump all excess fuel to safeguard the lives of all those passengers?"

To which a King's kid responds, "Why not ask the pilot?"

A King's kid is a reporter—not an explainer. This book is a reporting of some of the unlikely things that happen when a King's kid follows the instructions in the Manufacturer's Handbook—instead of kowtowing to his EIB.

Foreword

All my life I have marveled that, in His teachings, Jesus derived much of His imagery from everyday human life and activity. To the fishermen, He said, "I will make you fishers of men." To the baker, "The kingdom of heaven is like leaven." To the gardener, "The kingdom of heaven is like a grain of mustard seed."

However, in modern times, many of our "city kids" do not understand the language of the old "country boys." I once heard of a boy from a great city who visited a farm for the first time. He saw the farmer milking the cow, and pointing to the pail, asked, "What do you do with that?" When he was told that the cow was supplying them with milk, he promptly stated, "We don't drink cows' milk, we only drink dairy milk." I once asked a Sunday school class, "What do we mean when we sing 'Bringing in the Sheaves'? Not one had ever seen a sheaf of wheat, and so no one knew what the song was all about.

Some years ago, when I first met my good friend, Harold Hill, the electrical engineer, and heard his testimony, I was amused at his engineering terminology. Later, I called it his "engineering theology" when I found that his testimony and teaching had made a great impact on a friend of mine who was much more at home in the mechanical field than in the agricultural field. I saw that the Lord continues to speak through His servants in contemporary language, and I wished Harold would put his testimony in writing. My wish is now fulfilled in *How to Live Like a King's Kid*.

This book will be a great blessing to many. I recommend it especially to those who complain that the things of the Spirit are foolishness to them. Here you will discover the testimony of a man born of the Spirit, a story brightly colored with the jargon of mechanical engineering. May God bless everyone who reads this book.

David J. du Plessis

Introduction

It is a happy privilege to be able to write an introductory word to any book written by Harold Hill.

I met Hal a few months after he began his spiritual pilgrimage, and we have had a close and joyous association in the subsequent years. Hal is an authentic Christian witness who not only says, "It is written," he also says, "It has happened to me."

The author of this book is exceedingly strong on personal experience because Jesus Christ is very personal to him, and he has learned to go directly to God for himself. On the other hand, he has been saved from the erroneous assumption that personal experience is a license for private interpretation of the Scripture. His faith has been tried in the fires of deep involvement with the lives of others, both Christian and non-Christian. He has learned to walk in that happy balance between the "universal" and the "particular."

As is true with most people who are acutely spiritually attuned, Hal Hill has eyes to see "an Angel standing in the sun," that is, the outward order is a visible sign of the kingdom of heaven. Consequently, he describes the life of the Spirit in terms of a mind trained in the natural sciences. The Bible becomes *The Manufacturer's Handbook,* and vital union with Jesus is expressed as a "power hook-up."

Disciplined obedience to the laws of God in the natural world is undeniably linked to the manifestation of supernatural power in Hal's life. He believes in the reality of heaven but is not looking for an escape hatch.

Harold Hill makes no attempt to be a systematic theologian. He writes from the perspective of a contemporary businessman who made the discovery that the Incarnation meant that God loved him and was able to reach him where he was, to take him as he was, and make of him what he ought to be — a child of God, "saved by grace through faith."

Through the anointing of the Holy Spirit, this book will be made meat and drink to the reader who hungers and thirsts after righteousness. The writer is not saying that it has to happen to anyone else in the same way it happened to him. He is saying, however, "If God can do this for me, only heaven knows what He can do for anyone else."

May the blessings of our Lord continually abide with the one who writes and with those who read.

Tommy Tyson
Chapel Hill, NC

HOW TO LIVE LIKE A KING'S KID

is for you

if you want to lay hold of

the abundant life

Jesus came to give you

1
How a King's Kid Lives

Three days before Christmas, I was in an airplane coming back from an assignment at the space tracking station on Coopers Island, Bermuda. We had flown into the New York area and were still circling around. There was nothing unusual about that. Air traffic over New York is generally pretty heavy, and sometimes it takes as much as ten or fifteen minutes to get clearance for landing. But on this particular day, we had already circled for thirty minutes when the captain came back and said, rather *un*confidently, "We're having a little trouble with our landing gear, but we hope to have it corrected in a few minutes."

The few minutes passed, and a few minutes more, and the captain came back again and told us how to brace ourselves for a landing without wheels.

The plane was scheduled to take off immediately for London. I knew we had a full load of fuel for transatlantic travel, and it is illegal to dump fuel over the New York area. That particular kind of plane—the jet prop—nearly always catches fire when it drags the runway, landing without wheels. We were stuck with an almost certain firebomb.

My first reaction to the news was, "Hallelujah! This is graduation day! Lord, make it quick and easy."

It would be quick, all right, no question about that. It could be very fatal very suddenly for all of us. But did I feel torment? Not a bit. Actually I felt a sense of anticipation. This would be a new experience. I'd been shouting about victory in death for a long time, and I was about to check it out. Praise the Lord!

Then the Holy Spirit brought me up short. *Hill, you're being just as selfish and self-centered as ever. How about the other people on this plane—the pagans who don't know Me, the guys full of all that counterfeit Christmas cheer from the bottle? Think of them—the condition they're in. Graduation won't be such a celebration for them.*

"I'm sorry, Lord," I said, and I went to interceding. "Lord," I prayed, "I need to know what to pray for—I guess I need a word of knowledge." By the Holy Spirit's gift of a word of knowledge, God is able to provide us with information by supernatural means. He always has all the facts, and He can give us the ones we need when we pray in the Spirit and ask Him for them. Knowledge is not always necessary to us, but when it is necessary, the Holy Spirit will supply it without fail.

As I prayed in the Spirit, praying in tongues that my natural mind could not understand or control, I was given a readout—supernatural knowledge by way of a picture as clear as a TV picture. I saw an X ray of the whole landing system of that aircraft—hydraulic actuators, cylinders, pumps, everything. And I *saw* what was wrong with the landing gear. All the oil had leaked out of the hydraulic system. Naturally the wheels couldn't come down—there was no vehicle there to accomplish it.

Interesting as it was to see what was wrong, it would be even better to get it fixed. And so I prayed, "Lord, fix it. Please replenish the oil in that drained-dry system so that the landing gear will work." And then, as I continued to pray in the Spirit, I saw the heavenly hydraulic fluid, the holy oil of the Spirit, run all through the airplane's system. As it became filled, the wheels went down—when we were within ten feet of the ground. It was a perfect landing—on a runway lined with firetrucks, ambulances, and movie cameras. They had it all set up for the biggest fire in the history of Kennedy Airport.

As we rolled to a stop, the captain came back to speak to the passengers one more time. He was white as a sheet, his voice shaky.

"Folks," he said, "I have no idea what happened." If he'd asked me, I could have told him, but he didn't ask me, just tried to explain it to himself as he stood there wagging his head in disbelief. "Our instruments showed the fluid had leaked out of the mechanism," he said, "so there was no way to get the wheels down, no brakes, no steering—" He stopped to swallow, hard. "It was impossible, but the wheels came down anyway, just in time, and I was able to reverse the props and stop us just before we would have crashed through the administration building."

I could see we were parked in front of the administration building, where we had no business being, except that was the only place where there were no planes in the way of ours. There wasn't a penny's worth of damage to anything—and Jesus had done it all. All He needed was one intercessor who was already prayed up and praised up. There wouldn't have been time for me to get into a gear of praising and trusting God if I'd been out of it. And God honored my prayer with a miracle.

I'd like to see the logsheet of BOAC airlines for that particular day to see what they entered in the logbook. It couldn't have been a usual matter-of-fact statement. It had to be something that sounded weird, because the Holy Spirit had been in charge of the whole situation.

That same day, I found myself temporarily marooned at the airport. The connecting plane for Baltimore—the one on which I had reservations—hadn't shown up, and I wanted to get home. It being the Christmas season, there were millions of people on the move. And there was no earthly reason why my needs should have priority over anyone else's. But God had just showed me what He could do when I trusted Him, so as I waited, I rejoiced, praying, "Lord, when You can get me out of an almost sure-death situation like that, You can certainly get me to Baltimore with no trouble at all."

Certain that God had something in store for me, though I

didn't know what or how, I went through the motions of checking all the ordinary resources. I called the bus lines. They were booked full. I checked all the airlines. There was no flight with space for me. There was no need to get on the waiting list—there were hundreds of names on it already.

I said, "Lord, I've done everything I know to do. I'm out of things to try. So I give up." And then I listened for His instructions. He told me to walk down to the boarding gate. Now, you never do that. You always wait at the ticket counter. But I didn't argue with the Lord. I said, "Yes, Lord," and walked down to the gate to see what He had for me there. I knew He wouldn't have me walk down to the gate for nothing.

At the gate, there just *happened* to be a plane loading for Washington, with an intermediate stop at Baltimore. Many people were on the waiting list. I knew that. There was no earthly way I could get on that flight, of course, but I stood there, praising God, really being joyful for the fix I was in. In the midst of my rejoicing, I heard them paging a Mr. So and So. Then finally, "Last call for Mr. So and So." It was take-off time, and he hadn't shown up.

The gatekeeper didn't go through the usual procedures to let the first stand-by on the list take Mr. So and So's place. There wasn't time for that. He just looked at me and asked, "Do you want to go to Baltimore?"

I said, "Yes, sir."

He said, "Come on."

I climbed aboard, he closed the gate, and off we went.

In the natural, the events of that day couldn't have happened. But I had been a King's kid aboard that about-to-crash airplane. And later, I had been a King's kid waiting at the gate of the filled-up flight. And King's kids don't have to settle for the natural. They don't even have to settle for second best. King's kids get special treatment. They can live like King's kids—as long as they look to the King.

God says, *Let everything that hath breath praise Me.* The EIB says, "Wait until I catch my breath," and never does.

God says, *Read my Word, do it, and report on the results.* The EIB says, "But what about this? What if that? Suppose so and so?" and is a hearer only, and not a doer. The EIB makes of us the split-heads of James 1:8, double-minded men, and snatches defeat from certain victory.

God says, *Except ye become as a little child—* and the EIB scoffs, "Oversimplification!"

God says, *Prove me now,* and the EIB stalls, "Let me figure it out first and see if it fits into my theology."

This EIB principle stands out in Acts 4:13 where after seeing the disciples ministering charismatically with signs following, the Educated Idiots of the religious world were bugged because no one among the King's kids had a PhD.

And so, even now, as you read chapter one of this book, you might even detect the tendency in yourself to ask, "Why didn't the BOAC pilot fly out to sea and dump all excess fuel to safeguard the lives of all those passengers?"

To which a King's kid responds, "Why not ask the pilot?"

A King's kid is a reporter—not an explainer. This book is a reporting of some of the unlikely things that happen when a King's kid follows the instructions in the Manufacturer's Handbook—instead of kowtowing to his EIB.

2
How to Succeed in Everything

I didn't always know about being a King's kid. Although I had a Christian mother, I grew up acknowledging no God but my own head. I didn't know the truth of Isaiah 1:5, "The whole head is sick," until my own head proved it to me when I was forty-eight years old.

I must have been no more than ten when I read a book on the physics of electricity. It fascinated me, and as I read, I knew my life's work would be in that area. And so I set out to be an engineer, and laid a course of action for my life which embodied some very clear-cut goals. In the first place, I wouldn't be just an ordinary engineer. I would be a *chief* engineer. I would earn a hundred dollars a week—that was a fabulous amount of money in those days. I would travel a lot, have a lovely family, be successful, and be completely happy, of course.

In the beginning, everything worked out beyond my fondest hopes.

I finished high school at age fourteen—I wasn't a genius,

but I was in a hurry. I knew what I wanted, and was able to skip some grades in school. I couldn't wait for those dumb kids, as I called them, kids who were still wondering whether they wanted to be firemen, or policemen, or street-sweepers. I was ready to get the show on the road, to make my million and be happy.

I reached my first goal—to be chief engineer—at the age of twenty-eight. At thirty-two, I was promoted to executive vice president. At age thirty-five, I was director of engineering, director of sales, director of several corporations. I had an excellent salary—considerably better than my dreamed-of one hundred dollars a week—plus a ten percent commission before taxes. When the war came, our profits measured in barrels of green stuff.

I was clearly a success—a big fat empty miserable success.

No one had told me that success could kill me. They didn't tell me that executives have their first heart attack at age fifty-two. They didn't tell me you'd better have psychiatrists on your payroll when you get to be vice-president of your company, because your first nervous breakdown is right around the corner. They didn't tell me that you lose all your friends the day you're made active head of your company, because everybody is out to steal your job and undermine your reputation. And when you're made president—the top of the totem pole—you're an isolated nobody, an untouchable—you've had it. You can't trust anybody. They're all after your job. You're afraid, and your pagan life is utterly devoid of meaning.

Mine was.

One day I sat in my plush office thinking about the futility of my life. Deep down inside, something told me, "There's got to be something better." And I knew that the "something better" wasn't to be found in more success. Success was for the birds. As a young engineer, I had worked for a time for a British concern, and my boss was a British nobleman. I had lived with success, traveled with the Rolls Royce crowd, the Jet Set, the beautiful people. They were all as sick, as miserable, as empty, frustrated, going-nowhere-and-coming-from-nowhere people as I was.

I was already a compulsive drinker, drinking in a vain effort to alleviate the frustration of success and the boredom which are inevitably the lot of one who lives for self-gratification, as I did. I had no real purpose in life. My beautiful home and family, my successful business, my high professional standing? Worthless. That I was on the right boards of directors and appeared at all the right meetings and belonged to the right golf clubs and country clubs and yacht clubs and bridge clubs and chess clubs? Equally worthless.

Down inside me, where I really lived, there was no plush office, no swanky club, no dignity, no worth. I was a one-man slum—a dirty, drab, empty corpse, worn-out at forty-five.

There was nothing left but to make my corpsehood official. I would kill myself, and then they could bury me and be done with it. That day, I took enough poison to wipe out the whole neighborhood, put it in a tall tumbler, mixed it with a quantity of Four Roses, poured a few drops of water on top to thin it down, and drained the glass.

3
How to Stop Drinking

A success at everything else I had ever attempted, I goofed at suicide. It must have been the water that turned my stomach. The poison bounced. It came back up.

A few days later—maybe a few weeks, I'm not clear about the timing, because everything was buried in a red haze of alcohol—I came home about 4:00 A.M. with my usual Friday relaxation—two-fifths inside me. Being bored to death with life, and having failed at my first suicide attempt, I had decided to end my life in a slower, less dramatic way by drinking myself to death as painlessly as possible. I didn't like pain, and I was one big hurt, all over. That Good Friday night of 1951, I hurt so bad I cried out, "God, help me!"

And He did.

The next week He sent me to a meeting of Alcoholics Anonymous. I looked around me and wondered, "What am I doing in this place? I certainly don't belong here. Why, I'll probably get worse if I associate with these people." But much to my surprise, as the evening wore on, for the first time in my life, I saw people with something that I wanted, a kind of peace, something that looked like real joy.

They assured me that if my need was deep enough and that if I was sufficiently aware of it, God would make Himself real to me at the level of my need. They encouraged me not to try to understand God, just to accept Him for who He says He is. They said He would reveal Himself to me in His written word and that He would take over my life as I relinquished it to Him. He would become what I was inadequate to be for myself. He would be my Manager, if I would let Him.

A Manager was just exactly what I needed. That night, I asked God to take over the management of my life in just one area—my drinking. At first, I wondered how He could do it. It seemed kind of hopeless.

The AA members asked me, "Can you go for a day without a drink?"

I assured them I could not. No way.

"Can you go for an hour without a drink?"

"I doubt it." I was being as honest as I knew how to be, and an hour is a long time when you're as addicted as I was.

But they didn't seem at all discouraged or about to give up. "How about five minutes? Can you go for five minutes without a drink?"

"I believe I can."

"All right, then," they said. "That is your program—just five minutes at a time. Don't take a drink for five minutes."

When the shakes and other withdrawal symptoms set in hard about five o'clock the next afternoon, I tried postponing the first drink five minutes at a time, and arrived home sober—instant results through God's program of AA. I had experienced, firsthand, the power of God, without even knowing that His first name is Jesus. That came later.

And by God's grace, one day at a time for the past twenty-three years, I've not found it necessary to take a drink.

To stop drinking proved relatively simple, but after all, my drinking was a minor problem—the symptom of a much worse problem, the whole problem of my self. It remained, magnified, because I wasn't ready to trust God to manage my self for me.

During the next two years, the problem of my self, my cold sober self, got worse and worse. And I couldn't even take a drink to journey into oblivion once in a while, to forget. I had to face the problem of me—day after unending day.

All the while, I was watching one of the men I saw regularly at AA meetings. I couldn't figure him out. I classed him as a peasant, because he was just an ordinary engineer with Bethlehem Steel, and I had my own business. But there was a glow about him. He had a voluble wife, but he was never disturbed. He had more children than I did, but he was a lot less bothered than I was.

I knew the man had problems, but he never looked as if they got *to* him down inside. As a matter of fact, after two years, his beautiful serenity was such a contrast to my own ugly misery that it was about to drive me crazy.

And so, at one o'clock in the morning, two years after I first met him, I knocked on Ed's front door. When he opened it, I said, "Ed, whatever this is that you have, I've got to have it." I had finally admitted to myself that he had the kind of reality I needed.

4
How to Get Out of Quick-Mud

My friend Ed said, "Come in," and then he began to explain reality to me.

We had read Scripture together a number of times before, but that night Ed got personal and said he was able to be so free because he had confessed his sins, and the blood of Jesus had scrubbed him, cleaned him.

In the past, I hadn't liked to hear about the blood of Jesus, and when anyone had mentioned sin to me, my gizzard rolled over and tried to cover up the awful spidery mess knotted in the pit of my stomach.

But that night, I was desperate enough to keep listening. And Ed showed me the verse in John where Jesus said, "I am the way, the truth, and the life, and if you want to know your Heavenly Father, you've got to do it through Me or not at all."

Always before, I had objected to that verse, asking, "But what about the Hindus, and what about the Buddhists, and what about—"

But that night, it was as if God interrupted, saying, *Forget about them. What about you?*

Ed asked me, "How about it? Do you want Jesus—or don't you—on His terms—without quibbling?"

I was miserable enough to say yes, and near as I can remember, I prayed something like this:

"Lord Jesus, if You are really here, and my friend Ed seems to think so, please make Yourself real to me, right now."

It wasn't much of an invitation, but it was all the invitation He needed. I felt as if He had opened me up, moved inside of me, zippered me back around Him, and turned me on, installing perfect peace and washing out forty-eight years of filth. He made me know that I was right with God forever, and that my record was gone, that all my sins were as far away from me as the East is from the West, that He had buried them in a sea of forgetfulness. And that in heaven, the seas would be no more—that's how all gone my sins were, all the muck that had been threatening to swallow me forever. I was forgiven.

As a boy growing up in the country, I used to do a lot of exploring with my brother. There was one particular marsh everybody warned us to stay away from. It had quick-mud, a peculiar kind of mud that instead of resisting the movement of a body through it, tends to draw the body to the bottom. If you fall into quick-mud, and there's nobody to help you, you'll go right down out of sight at the rate of about one inch per minute.

18

The marsh being a no-no, naturally my brother and I were honor-bound to explore it thoroughly.

We were out hopping the bogs one day when I slipped into the mud and began to sink. I was about forty inches long, and that meant in about forty minutes, I'd be suffocated, choked to death by the quick-mud. All of me that would be left would be a little dimple on the surface of the sticky black goo.

I was scared to death, too terrified even to cry.

Recently, the Lord brought forcibly to my mind all the religions, the philosophies, and the cults in which I had been involved in my pagan days, and showed me what they had to offer when I was sinking in the filthy black muck which represented the sin in my life:

Confucius said, "It is better to stay away from such places, young man." And having delivered that wonderful advice, he went on his way and left me to sink.

Buddha said, "Let that be a lesson to you, my boy," and I sank down further. I had been a Buddhist and knew that these things were supposed to be lessons, so when I reincarnated the next time around, I might have a better trip.

Mohammed sighed and said, "It is the will of Allah," and I sank deeper.

Christian Science said, "It is only an error in your thinking. You're not really in trouble. You're just thinking wrong." I had been a Christian Scientist, but right thinking hadn't cured my alcoholism. So I sank another inch, and I didn't have many inches to spare.

19

The Hindus told me, "Better trip next incarnation. You got a bum trip, coming as a flea this time. You might come as a fly, next go round." The filthy black ooze sucked me deeper.

The evolutionist told me, "All you need is more time. Time cures everything, my boy." But I was worse off with every passing minute.

Yoga told me, "Transcend your problem." I had tried. I had sat and I had contemplated so long I got bored with the whole thing and wished a daisy would grow out of my navel just to relieve the monotony. Now my navel had sunk out of sight. I'd never see it again.

Unity had said, "All you need is to realize more love." But how are you going to love yourself out of a swamp of quick-mud?

A fortune-teller told me, "Consult the zodiac. The stars have the answer." But the stars weren't shining that day, and so I sank deeper.

Darwin said, "It is the survival of the fittest. If you are fit, you will survive." That's what I was afraid of. Sinking another inch, I proved my unfitness for anything except being buried alive.

Aristotle smiled and said, "My boy, just know thyself." That was the trouble. I knew myself—headed for the bottom of the mudpile.

Plato said, "Truth is the answer. Just seek the truth." But he wasn't talking about tangible truth, a living truth, and truth in his terms meant that I was about to be annihilated.

Zoroaster said, "Use your willpower." But I had used mine all up, and it had availed me nothing. I was about finished.

A headshrinker, a psychiatrist, said, "Don't feel guilty. All you need is to go out and do some more sin." But I was in such bondage there was no way to go out anywhere or do anything.

I had also tried Spiritual Frontiers, New Thought, Moral Rearmament, Edgar Cayce, and all the rest. None of them helped at all. I sank deeper and deeper until I was almost totally lost.

There was no religion, no philosophy, that I had not looked into. All claiming to be different, they were all the same, worthless, leaving me in my miserable, empty, inane, dreary, drab, stinking corpsehood.

But then Jesus came by, and He said, *I'm the way, I'm the only way. Just give Me your hand.*

I didn't argue, "But what about the others?" I just gave Him my hand, and He gave me His. He hauled me out of that filthy black mud and set my feet on solid rock and washed the mud away.

No, it wasn't exactly Jesus Himself who physically took me from the mud that day when I was a little boy so nearly gone. But somehow, at the very last minute, when I was holding my breath because I sensed my next breath would be my last one, He sent two strangers through the woods to pull me to safety. I never learned the names of the strangers. I hadn't seen them before, and I haven't seen them since. But I wouldn't be surprised if the men who got me out were two angels, sent to deliver God's elect because I had a Christian mother who had consigned me to Jesus even before I was born.

On the day when I met Him in person, the day He pulled me out of the black muck of sin and washed me clean, I was no longer a little boy exploring the marsh with my brother. I was a grown man embarking on the greatest adventure anyone of any age could ever have—learning to live like a King's kid.

5
How to Start Over

When I got off my prayer bones in Ed's living room that night, I was a new creation in Christ Jesus. I could feel the newness. Suddenly all the hatred, the torment, the bitterness, and all the guilt were gone. II Corinthians 5:17-18 had set in, right while I waited. "If any man be in Christ, he is a new creature: old things are passed away; behold all things are become new. And all things are of God."

When I discovered how simple it was, I said, "There's got to be more to it than that. Don't I have to *do* something?"

Ed laughed. "There's more to it, all right," he said. "But that's the beginning. You start with the first things first." And then he quoted a Scripture to me: "To as many as received Him, to them He gave the power to become the sons of God." And then he said, "You're just a baby Christian now, Hill, but you've received Him, so now you have the power to become His son. You'll grow. God will start working on you."

He kind of chuckled again when he said that, as if he knew more than I could guess about the changes that were in store for me.

And Ed was right. Instantly and continuously and progressively, my life began to change. The instant part was the peace I had inside me all of a sudden instead of the torment I had been used to for so long. If that was all Jesus did for me, it would have been marvelous enough. It was great to know I didn't have to keep struggling to make enough Brownie points to get me into God's good graces and to keep me there. I could quit trying to pile up merits to offset the ratty things I had done all my life. It was wonderful not to have to feel guilty anymore. The blood of Jesus had washed me whiter than snow, and I knew it.

My friend Ed did say it would be helpful for me to go forward to receive a hand of fellowship from the local church, to make a public confession of my new faith in Jesus.

I was willing enough, but I always liked to know the reason for everything, so I asked him, "Why should I do that? How will that change anything?"

Ed shrugged his shoulders. "I don't know," he said, "but God recommends it, and I found it helpful."

So I went to his little Baptist church with him. And when the pastor invited anyone who wanted to, to come forward and make a public profession of faith—a confession with his mouth that he had faith in Jesus in his heart—I went forward and did it.

They scheduled a baptismal service for me right away, and I dutifully got wet all over, being immersed in the dunk tank. I didn't mind too much. The Bible said New Testament Christians were baptized by being immersed—that's what the word *baptizo* means—and if New Testament Christians did it, that was good enough for me. Besides, I read that Jesus was baptized by John in the River Jordan, and so baptism seemed a good thing for me if I was going to follow Him.

When I came up out of the water, I was disappointed. I didn't feel anything but wet. I thought I had done something pretty terrific, humbling myself in a little old country Baptist church like that. And I waited for a ball of fire to hit, but nothing happened, not then. Ed said the feelings would come later.

They did. And they still do.

I had read the Bible as part of my education, dragging through it. I had to force myself to read it because it was so deadly dull. This was the greatest book in all the world? I couldn't believe it. Then, the morning after I met Jesus personally in Ed's living room, I picked up the Bible, and when I had read just a verse or two, I wondered who had put new pages inside the cover. Somebody had tampered with my Bible. Why, it was brand-new, not dull at all, but tremendously exciting and so personal it was as if every line of it had been written just for me.

Finally it dawned on me—the Bible hadn't been rewritten, *I* had been rewritten, reborn, born again by the Spirit of

God. Jesus was alive in me.

Like Ed said, I was a baby Christian with power to become a son, but I was in the messy stage. But we don't throw babies away because they're messy. We wash them and feed them and train them.

And so the older Christians accepted me, and I began to grow as God fed me. More and more old things passed away and all things became new, and I began to know that all things are of God—because He says so.

6
How to Stop Gambling

In the beginning of my life as a new Christian, I could get away with anything, it seemed like. God provided all sorts of latitude. But then came a narrowing-down process, and the things of the world became less and less desirable to me. I didn't set out to give them up, they gave *me* up as time went along.

For as long as I could remember, I had been a poker addict. Try as I might, I couldn't get rid of the habit. Finally, I quite fighting it, and I said, "Lord, if I really belong to You completely, this gambling habit is Yours, not mine." I didn't ask Him to help me win games, but I did invite Him to go along, to sit in with me. I said, "Lord, if You like sitting in on poker games, that's Your privilege, because when I'm sitting in, You're sitting in. And if that's pleasing to You, fine. I'm going to forget all about." In other words, I stopped fighting my gambling habit, and I started loosing it to Him.

A weekend or two later, I went on a fishing trip with

several men, and we played a *lot* of poker. I won every game. I couldn't lose. It didn't matter what I did, I raked in every pot.

Normally, I would have been tickled to death. But as the pile of chips grew higher and higher in front of me, I became more and more miserable. I knew the men playing with me couldn't afford to lose. I was taking their rent money, their grocery money, money for their children's trips to the orthodontist. But when you're playing poker, you can't drop out for any such reasons as those. You're just stuck with it. That's the ethics of the game.

When that weekend was finally over, I was so sick at what I had done to the people that I said, "Lord, please Lord, I don't want to play poker anymore." The desire to gamble left me. I didn't have to leave it. I didn't have to fight it. It was gone.

I played poker only one more time, when I was on a business trip to Minneapolis with a group of pagans. I don't suppose any one of them had ever heard the Gospel. Not one of them had ever heard a Christian testimony.

I hadn't even planned to go on the trip until I got a definite direction from the Lord about it. He seemed to say, *Who's going to represent Me if you don't go?*

"All right, Lord," I told Him, "if You feel that way about it, I'll go."

And when the men invited me to play poker with them, I was about to excuse myself, but it seemed as if the Lord said, *Now just why do you think I brought you along on this trip? What's the matter all of a sudden? Are you too good to be seen in a poker game?*

"Lord," I argued, "I thought we were through with all that. *You* don't like it, do You?"

I imagined that I heard Him snorting at me, kind of indignant like. *Use your head, Hill. How are these people going to hear about Me in an inspirational way if you don't sit in on the game? They're always hearing about Me in a destructive way—profanity. Who's going to lift Me up in the right way so I can draw them to Myself?*

I understood then what He was getting at, and I thanked Him and sat in on the game. I don't even remember whether I won or lost. My mind wasn't on what happened with the cards, but on what was happening in the hearts of the other men. One of the players was a Jewish millionaire I'd known all my business life. That day, I had a chance to witness to him just a little bit—not a whole lot, but just to drop a few words. It didn't seem so important until a few days later when he returned from that business trip and blew his brains out. He might never have heard about God in a real, living way, if I hadn't been in that poker game. And who can say whether or not he might have turned to the living God in the last seconds of his consciousness and been saved?

God always knows what He's doing, and He works it all together for good when we trust Him.

7
How to Get More for Your Money

When I started being a Christian, since I was a scientist, and interested in maximum results, I began to read the Bible as the Manufacturer's Handbook. I saw it as the Originator of all things, God the Creator, the Manufacturer, speaking to His creation, His product, people, telling them how to use what He had made for them. And I said, "Lord, I'm going to try every principle You bring to my attention in this book. I'm going to experiment with it. Anything that works, I will do Your way. What shall I do first?"

There's no doubt in my mind that God heard, because almost immediately I ran head on into the biggest problem a Scotchman can encounter—tithing.

God said, *The first tenth belongs to Me.*

I said, "But Lord, I don't get the first tenth myself. You know they take a big bite out of your paycheck these days—withholding taxes, old age pension, hospital insurance, and all that." I thought it made sense to deduct all those things and then give God the first tenth of what was left.

I thought that was certainly generous of me and that God would appreciate it. Or maybe, if He didn't like it, He just wouldn't notice what I was up to.

I didn't know the Scripture that says everything is exposed to the eyes of Him with whom we have to do. And all that time, He was looking down inside of me, seeing this rationalizing, this holdout business.

After I had been doing this conniving kind of tithing about ten months, God began to show me that I wasn't trusting Him. I had one hand on my pocketbook for security and one hand on Jesus, and that was a rather precarious position.

One morning when I was trying to pray, I couldn't seem to make contact. All I could see were dollar signs floating through the air. After being uncomfortable as long as I could stand it, my pocketbook being the tenderest part of my anatomy, I thought I heard God say, *Who are you fooling? Who are you kidding? Certainly not Me. How about yourself?*

I was so relieved to hear from Him, I heaved a big sigh of relief and said, "Lord, from now on, You get the first tenth, the *whole* first tenth, before any deductions of any kind. I don't understand why You have to have all that. But I don't need to understand it. I'm just going to try it, trusting You."

I was satisfied, and I thought that would be the end of it. God was satisfied, too—wasn't He? But no, it seemed like He said something else, something about some unfinished business.

How about all this you've been holding out on Me for about ten months? How about that?

"Well," I said, feeling my Adam's apple bobbing up and down and hearing my voice squeak like an adolescent, "Well, Lord, but that's an awful lot of money."

He didn't say it wasn't. He didn't say anything else right then. He just left it up to me. But I couldn't stop asking myself, "Well, how about that? How about that?"

Finally I made Him a proposition. "Lord," I said, "I'll tell You what I'll do. I don't have it. But when I get it, I'll pay it." That completed the transaction. God took me at my word. He was satisfied—and I was satisfied. The carrying out of the proposition was only incidental, once I'd made the decision.

A couple of weeks later, I got a completely unexpected bonus check for double the amount I owed God. Half for me, and half for Him, as if to show me that if I'm stingy, He's not.

I was beginning to experience the truth of the Scripture in Malachi 3:10: "Bring ye all the tithes into the storehouse . . . and prove me now herewith, saith the Lord of hosts, if I will not open you the windows of heaven, and pour you out a blessing, that there shall not be room enough to receive it."

Actually, your paycheck is the receipt for the portion of your life that you give to your boss. When you grasp it and hold onto it, you're choking your own life to death. Holding onto your money is a symbol that you've not really relinquished your life to Jesus. But when you loose it on earth, it's loosed in heaven, and that opens the floodgates for God to pour out a blessing so big you won't have room to receive it all.

When God says, *Prove Me. Make Me prove what I'm talking about,* He's always inviting us, not to sacrifice, but to be obedient so He can bless us abundantly.

Every now and then, someone says to me, "When you talk about tithing, you're trying to put us back under the law." I used to think that, too. And when the preacher would say, "If you will tithe, your whole life will benefit," I'd say to myself, "Uh huh, you're just begging for money." I wasn't about to throw away a tenth of my income. But now I know God wants us to tithe for *our* benefit. It *is* more blessed, more beneficial, happier, to give than to receive. The law is our servant once we're born-again children of the King, living like King's kids.

God has set up a tithing principle, giving the first tenth to Him, in order to set us free from the bondage of our selves. It's the greatest thing that could happen to a Scotchman like me. In the old days when I went to church twice a year whether I needed it or not—Christmas Eve and Easter Sunday—when I put a dollar in the plate, I could feel the roots of it tearing at my gizzard. And you should have seen the lies on my income tax about what a quick spender I was in the church. It's a wonder they didn't catch me at it.

Now, they have me on the carpet just about every year, and I have the receipts and canceled checks to back my contributions up. What a marvelous opportunity I have with the Internal Revenue to tell them about Jesus every year! They're entitled to hear these things because they ask me questions, and I always end up asking them, "Sir, have you ever considered accepting Jesus as your Savior?"

What a relief it was when I opened my pocketbook and said, "Lord, it's *all* Yours. What part of it do You want me to put where?" It *is* all His. I'm just a channel for it, a steward. Not one penny of it is really mine. The Lord allows that part of it to come my way which I need, and my wants and my needs are coming closer together all the time, because it is all in the hands of Jesus, my Lord and Master.

I heard R. G. LeTourneau talk about this some years ago at a businessmen's retreat at Wheaton College. He told us that if he didn't give away ninety percent of his income, he'd be overrun with the green stuff. And I said, "I'd like to be overrun that way. Being a Scotchman, I'm built that way. And if it will work for him, it'll work for me." Today, I can't afford to stop at tithing, double tithing, triple tithing, because the eight-tenths or the seven-tenths go so much further than the ten-tenths ever did that there's no comparison.

A little while after I started doing it God's way, a man called one night and said, "Could I come over and talk to you about saving money on your mortgage?"

And I said, "No, I wouldn't be interested."

"You mean you don't want to save money?"

I said, "What Scotchman doesn't? But I don't happen to have a mortgage."

He thought I didn't know what the word "mortgage" meant, so he rephrased his question. "How much money do you owe on your home?" he said.

I said, "I knew what you meant the first time around, because I've been paying on one all my adult life, ever since I've been married and owned a home. But now I don't have a mortgage. As a matter of fact, I don't owe anybody any money."

He acted as if he didn't believe me. He said, "Do you know that only one out of eight hundred and some *thousand* homeowners do not have a mortgage?"

I said, "Well, if that's what you say, I believe it. That's your business. But I happen to be one of them."

"Well," he said, "how do you account for that?"

He had asked a question. He was entitled to an answer. And I said, "I'm glad you asked the question. All I did was begin to live God's way and live for Him and put Him first, and I began tithing and giving, and I don't owe any money on our home. Or on anything else. That's how I account for it."

He said, "Oh," and he hung up. And I felt sorry for him.

King's kids can give abundantly because they receive abundantly when they're living God's way. If you put yourself in a position to receive God's goodness, you don't have to settle for second best. You can be set free. You can live like a King's kid—if you follow the Manufacturer's Handbook.

8
How to Get Rid of an Aching Back

When I first became a Christian, I was in constant pain from a disintegrated spinal disk. X rays showed total pulverization, total destruction, the disk all ground up to a powder. The vertebrae were grinding on each other, pinching nerves, and my legs were numb and prickly. The doctor had told me that without surgery, in two years I'd be paralyzed from the waist down. I wanted relief from the excruciating pain, but surgery didn't appeal to me, and so I kept putting it off and putting it off.

Then I came across the promise of God in Mark 16:17-18: "These signs shall follow them that believe . . . In my name they shall lay hands on the sick, and they shall recover." Being such a new Christian, I was too dumb to doubt, and so I consulted every religious person in Baltimore about God's power to heal. I wanted to find somebody who would lay hands on me so I could recover, just like the Bible said.

But everybody brushed me off. They said, "Well, Hill,

39

you know that was canceled when the disciples died off. God doesn't do that kind of thing anymore. We have doctors and medicine now."

"Are you trying to tell me that God's power petered out when Peter petered out?" I asked them.

Well, that's what *they* said, but that's not what my Bible said. It said that Jesus was the same yesterday, today, and forever, *not* that He could heal people two thousand years ago but that He had gotten bored with it or gone into retirement just when I needed Him.

So I went to the Lord about it. I prayed, "Lord, if it's still true, please show me Your way. And if it's not true, scrub every reference to healing right out of the Book or send me a telegram from heaven saying it's no longer true. You've said it, and I believe it—but where is it?"

Not long afterward, God brought a healing evangelist to Baltimore. I got in the healing line in his big tent, he put his hands on my head and said, "Be healed in the name of Jesus Christ," and I got a new spine, right while I waited. Then I had a license to believe everything about healing in the Manufacturer's Handbook, not because somebody from some seminary said it was true or wasn't, but because I had the living proof in my back, a brand-new third lumbar disk.

That evangelist was Oral Roberts.

When I went back to my church healed after my pastor had guaranteed that such things no longer take place, his theology was somewhat disturbed. But my back was very comfortable. And they would have thrown me out except that I was a tither and they couldn't spare me.

For years I carried the confirmation of my healing in my back, but not long ago the Lord set it up for me to receive medical confirmation as well. I wasn't sick, I didn't know of any reason why I should see the doctor, but the Lord urged me strongly to make an appointment for a physical examination. Knowing that obedience is better than sacrifice, and that the General was sending orders to His soldier, I said, "Yes Sir," and made the appointment.

The doctor went through the usual preliminary list of questions, and finally he said, "Have you ever had a serious physical affliction?"

"Yes, I had a disintegrated spinal disk."

"Who was your doctor? Who made the diagnosis?"

I gave him the doctor's name, and he said, "Oh, yes. He's still in business in downtown Baltimore. Did he perform the surgery?"

"No."

"Who did?"

"Jesus."

The doctor looked at me as if he thought he hadn't heard right.

"Jesus was my surgeon," I said.

The doctor laid down his papers and pencil. "Tell me about it."

You never saw anyone so thirsty to hear about Jesus as that doctor. When I had finished my story, he said, "That's the most wonderful thing I ever heard of! I want to hear more about it later." Then we started back on the questions.

41

"Have you had any incurable diseases?"

"Yes, I'm an alcoholic."

"Tell me about it."

Wow! He couldn't hear enough. When I had finished telling him about that, the doctor said, "*That's* the most wonderful thing I ever heard of!" Then I knew that I was there by divine appointment, not because I needed any medical help, but to tell him about Jesus. He seemed to think that was all right, and he asked me to tell him some more about the healing of my disintegrated spinal disk.

"Have you had the thing X rayed since your healing?"

"No sir. I've paid all the X ray money I intend to. I have the healing, I don't need the pictures."

He said, "You know, I want to see what it looks like today. The cost will be covered by Medicare."

"You mean, the U.S. government will pay for pictures to back up the healing power of Jesus? Then count me in. If Uncle Sam is going to help me brag on Jesus, I'll go."

So he handed me a piece of paper and he said, "Call this lab and tell them I sent you. Tell them to look for a disintegrated or damaged disk in the lumbar region."

Well, I went to the X ray lab, and they put me under the camera and took the usual three shots, three different angles. They said, "Now wait here until we check and make sure that you haven't moved and blurred them." So I waited. And the technician came back and said, "Get under the camera another time." I got under. They took three more shots. She said, "Now wait."

They put me under that camera four times that day. They took twelve pictures, and they haven't found a damaged disk yet. God had made it whole.

Mark 16:17 is just as true as it ever was.

9
How to Fail at Witnessing

Seeing that the Manufacturer's Handbook knew what it was talking about in every area where I had tried it, I began to read the Bible with more and more interest. One day, I came across an interesting passage in the first chapter of the Book of Acts: "And being assembled together with them, [Jesus] commanded them that they should not depart from Jerusalem, but wait for the promise of the Father, which, saith he, ye have heard of me."

What was that promise? The Scripture went on to explain, "For John truly baptized with water; but ye shall be baptized with the Holy Ghost not many days hence."

"Baptized with the Holy Ghost?" What did that mean? I had never heard anything about it in the Baptist church, but I knew I had had some dealings with the Holy Ghost, because it says in I Corinthians 12:3 that "no man can say that Jesus is the Lord, but by the Holy Ghost." And I had claimed Him as my Lord.

I knew I had been baptized in water at the church because they had dunked me in the dunk tank. But what was this business about being baptized in the Holy Ghost? The Baptist church didn't seem to have anything to say on the subject. And when I asked Ed about it, he said, "Never heard of it," so I just shoved my question to a back burner of my mind and let it simmer there for a while.

I was satisfied that for all intents and purposes I had my reservations up yonder that I was going to pick up one of these days. Jesus had paid the whole tab for me, and since I'd said yes to Him, He would never turn me away. If He'd never lost one that the Father had placed in His hands—except for the one that had to be lost—He couldn't lose me either.

I was safe enough, but I kept getting the impression from the Bible and from the Baptist church that I was supposed to tell other people about Jesus so I could take some of them with me when I went to heaven. I tried to tell others about Him, but I just couldn't. I was so tonguetied, I couldn't speak before a group of just one person.

I enrolled in a seminary course in witnessing in one of the Baltimore churches. But it didn't help either, and after a couple of mechanized sessions, I threw the textbooks into the garbage can. I said, "Lord, there's got to be a better way of witnessing than the six-point Baptist program of pushing doorbells." Every time I pushed a doorbell, I'd pray there'd be no one at home. It was soul-winning in reverse. I was scared to death.

The ones who did show up on those dreary Sunday afternoons generally had a hangover, and they scowled at me and said, "Well, what do you want?"

I'd put on my best Sunday smile and say, with all the enthusiasm I could muster, "I'm Harold Hill from the Baptist church."

They'd give me a so-what stare, and say, "Oh, go away. We don't want you. Go away."

And I'd feel disgusted with myself, just as they had, and I'd apologize for bothering them and hang my head and walk away. I'd report back to the church and say, "I've tried, but it's no use. I just don't have any power to witness."

And when I asked them about the verse I found in Acts 1:8 where Jesus promised we'd get power to be witnesses when the Holy Ghost came upon us, they assured me that there was only one measure of the Holy Spirit available to Christians today, and that was the one I'd received in Ed's living room the night I was saved. That was all I'd ever get, they said, and then they walked away, shaking their heads at my stupidity and wondering why I was so all-fired curious about something in the word of God that they'd passed over without noticing all their lives.

But my curiosity had simmered on the back burner long enough, and out of my absolute misery in trying to witness, I really dug into the Scriptures, just as I had done when the church people had told me there was no such thing as God healing anybody in the twentieth century.

I didn't just read the Bible about this Baptism that was supposed to give me power to witness, I got down on my prayer bones, too. And pretty soon, what had been simmering on a back burner of my mind had come to a full rolling boil on the front of the stove.

10
How to Know the Truth about Baptisms

Approaching my study systematically and prayerfully, in I Corinthians 12:13 I read, "For by one Spirit are we all baptized into one body." I was sure this was talking about salvation, the baptism *of* or *by* the Holy Spirit where He baptizes us into membership in the Body of Christ. By this baptism, we all become members of His Body equally, Jew, or Greek, Gentile, heathen, whatever. We have all been made to drink into one Spirit. We're born again and made members of His Body by this baptism *by* the Holy Spirit. The Holy Spirit does the baptizing. We're the candidate, and the Body of Jesus is the element that becomes our dwelling place. That's the first baptism—the one that happened for me in my friend Ed's living room.

In my second baptism, the minister of the Baptist church officiated to dump me in the dunk tank. He explained that this baptism in water would not *cause* me to be saved—I was saved when I believed in my heart and confessed with my

49

mouth that Jesus was Lord—but water baptism was a witness to the world that I was a born-again Christian.

As I thought about it, I realized that something *had* happened to me when I was baptized in water. I think it had to do with drowning some of my arrogance and pride. My six-foot-two frame being manhandled by a little pastor, who couldn't have been over four feet fourteen or thereabouts, required some humility on my part. I really wasn't on my head to do it, and the lingering spirit of rebellion in me had to be belted, knocked out of the ballpark. Anytime I give in and surrender and subject myself to any other person, especially when I don't want to, I make an opportunity for the spirit of rebellion in me to be killed out a little bit more. Submitting to one another is a marvelous principle, and I've found that in practice it's highly beneficial.

In reading the Scriptures about water baptism, I ran across one in the second chapter of Colossians that was worth chewing on. It comes through very clearly in the Amplified Version of the New Testament: "In Him also you were circumcised with a circumcision not made with hands, but in a spiritual circumcision performed by Christ by stripping off the body of the flesh, the whole corrupt, carnal nature with its passions and lusts. Thus were you circumcised when you were buried with Him in your baptism. . . . "

That Colossians Scripture was clearly saying that *while* I was being baptized in water, Jesus stripped away my old sinful nature. If that was true—and I believed it was—my baptism in water was a whole lot more significant than just being a witness to the world that I was born again. The time and place of my baptism in water was the actual time and place when Jesus did an important work inside of me.

If these first two baptisms were so important, the third must be important too, I reasoned, or Jesus wouldn't have made it the subject of His last words to His disciples before He went up to heaven.

This third baptism, according to the Bible, was the Baptism *of* Jesus, the one He Himself would perform, baptizing us in the Holy Spirit. I found it mentioned in all four of the Gospels and right off, first thing, in the Book of Acts. The Scriptures in the first three Gospels were identical to one another:

"And He shall baptize you with the Holy Ghost and fire" (Matt. 3:11; Mark 1:8; Luke 3:16).

And John said, "Upon whom thou shalt see the Spirit descending, and remaining on him [that was Jesus], the same is he which baptizeth with the Holy Ghost" (John 1:33).

In Acts 1:5, just before He ascended into heaven, Jesus said, "Ye shall be baptized with the Holy Ghost not many days hence. . . . And ye shall receive *power,* after that the Holy Ghost is come upon you: and ye shall be witnesses unto me both in Jerusalem, and in all Judaea, and in Samaria, and unto the uttermost part of the earth."

This was the Baptism my church had never heard of, or

didn't believe existed, or thought was not for today, but I knew it was what I needed to be a witness.

I laid my Bible on the bed, got on my knees alongside of it, and said, "Lord, if these Scriptures are *not* for today, send me a telegram from heaven. Tell me to tear 'em out, and I'll tear 'em out. But until You do, they remain, and I'm going to find out how to work them, because I want to receive the power to be Your witness, and I know You want me to."

After I had prayed, I remembered that at the Oral Roberts' meeting where I was healed of my bad back, I had heard of a place called the Koinonia Foundation. It was the headquarters of C.F.O., at Pikesville, Maryland, and was not far from where I lived. And so a few weeks later, on a Sunday afternoon, I went over to see what the Koinonia Foundation was all about. I thought I was going just out of curiosity, but it was really the Spirit of the Lord leading me.

11
How to Be Baptized in the Holy Spirit

Most of the staff was out on assignments that day. But there was one young man named Jim in attendance, and he had time to spend with me.

I told him I was hungry for the power to be a witness, that I was hungry to share Jesus with others. I told him I had come out of the world of darkness, the world of top management, the world of industry, where we all drank ourselves to death if we were fortunate enough to do that before we disintegrated by heart attack or nervous breakdown. I had met Jesus, and so I had an answer for my colleagues in the business world, and I longed to share it with them, but I just couldn't. I couldn't tell them about Jesus. I was simply bottled up and tonguetied. I had no freedom to communicate Jesus. As a matter of fact, I had a serious block in my ability to communicate anything, and had had it since I was quite young. In college, I couldn't stand up to recite. I used to get low marks for my participation in class, even though I knew the answers, because I just could not communicate.

And so Jim witnessed to me that day about the power of the Holy Spirit to communicate God's love to others, and we sat out there on the back patio at the Koinonia place and he explained to me the meaning of the verses I had read in the New Testament.

He told me how the church at Ephesus had lacked power, and Paul went down to find out why. "Have you received the Holy Ghost since you believed?" he asked them. And they told him they had never heard of such a thing. Then Paul laid hands on them, and they received the Holy Ghost.

I knew he was talking about what I needed, because the Spirit within me witnessed to his testimony.

After he had explained all the Scriptures to me, Jim said, "Would you like for me to pray for you to receive this Baptism in the Holy Spirit from Jesus? Are you a candidate for His Baptism?"

And I said, "I'm a candidate for anything that Jesus has to offer me."

And then he asked me one more question, "Do you want everything God has for you *on His terms*?"

I said, "I certainly do."

He came around behind my chair, and laid his hands on my head. He prayed a simple prayer in English: "Baptize Harold in Your Holy Spirit, Lord. Take over his life. Make him a witness. Take full charge of his affairs. And Lord, if he's not sure he wants You to do it, do it anyhow. Now, Lord, I thank You for baptizing my brother in Your Holy

Spirit, for equipping him with all the gifts he'll need to serve You. Amen."

Then, while his hands were still on my head, he started praying in some other language. I didn't know what it was— just that it wasn't English. He was from Lumberton, North Carolina, and I suspected that he didn't know very many foreign languages, but this one—whatever it was—sounded beautiful.

That was the end of it. I waited for something to happen— power to surge through me, bells to ring, angel music to sound forth, fire to rest upon my head, but nothing happened as far as I could tell, except that I had a general feeling of freedom, of more peace than I'd ever known before.

I said to Jim, "I don't feel very different, really."

He said, "Wait a minute. Did you get saved because you felt something? Or because you believed God's word? It's the same way with any gift that God has for His people. You receive by faith and go and act like you have it, and you'll find that you have."

I took him at his word, and said, "Thank You, Jesus, for baptizing me in Your Holy Spirit."

Jim advised me to go home and read the Bible and praise God. "Don't stop praising Him," he said.

All the way home, I had a funny feeling of anticipation that something was about to happen. I went to bed, and during the night, something did happen. I'll not go into details, because then you'd look for an experience just like mine. And God has your own ready-made.

At any rate, when I woke up, I thought I must have been dreaming. "That was quite a dream," I thought. And then I knew it wasn't a dream, because Acts 1:8 was real—it was still there in my Bible. And the power was upon me. It was all over me, like tremendous waves of electricity, like waves of the energy of heaven. And that's exactly what it was. My tongue was loosed. I began to praise Jesus. I could say, "Praise Jesus. Thank You, Jesus, for my salvation. Thank You, Jesus, for eternal life. Thank You, Jesus, for You. Hallelujah!"

And right away I could tell something else was different, too. Once upon a time I had prayed, confessing I didn't have any love for other people and asking Jesus to let me know His love for them, to let it flow through me. When I got up that morning, feeling God's power all over me, I felt His love, too—for everybody. It was like liquid love, pouring over me, and I loved everybody I could think of with the very love of God Himself.

I barely touched the ground that day. The power and the love became so intense, I said, "Lord, can You turn it down a little bit, not too much, but just enough so that I can stay on this earth to find out what's going on?"

I knew I had received the Baptism in the Holy Spirit, and I could hardly wait to see if the power I felt would really work when I tried to witness.

12
How to Witness with Great Effect

A few days after my Baptism in the Holy Spirit, God sent me to the worst pagan I had ever known. I'd known him for years, and he used to fly into a rage when the name of Jesus was mentioned. That day, he looked me over, and said, "You're different."

I said, "I am?" I knew I was different inside, but I didn't know the difference showed outside already.

"Yeah," he said. "What happened to you?"

The Spirit inside me said, *Tell him about Jesus.*

Old Slue Foot was cackling in my ear. "Yeah, tell him," he said, "and he'll punch you in the nose so fast—"

I really thought he would, but I was empowered by the Holy Spirit, and I couldn't *not* tell him about Jesus. I began with simple words, telling exactly what had happened to me, and he just stood there, drinking it in, his eyes getting bigger and bigger. He was literally transfixed by the power of God.

After we'd been talking for five or ten minutes, he said,

"What do I have to do to get saved?" and I nearly collapsed.

Well, he did get saved. Blair Reed is his name. And he gave up his contracting business and went to North Carolina where for fifteen years or so he has run a home for alcoholics, the House of Prayer. He's a great disciple of Jesus Christ, and he has introduced thousands to the Lord. Blair got saved when the power of the Holy Spirit made me a witness.

Before I met Jesus as my Baptizer in the Holy Spirit, my witnessing didn't give the Lord a chance to run interference for me, to pick out and prepare the hearts of those to whom I was to speak about Him. No wonder I was such a colossal failure, barging in under my own feeble steam, thinking *I* would win someone for Him. I only turned them off, time after time. After my Baptism, however, I understood that *I* couldn't save anybody, that salvation was Jesus' job, and that He would open the doors where He wanted me to witness. I learned to wait for a question, wait for an open door, and then I could know He was backing me up. The Scripture He gave me was, "I send you forth as sheep in the midst of wolves. Be sly as serpents and harmless as doves." I soon found that it worked, as long as I was depending on *Him* to accomplish His purpose, and not trying to do it myself.

I was crossing the ocean one night on a business trip to England, and sitting next to me in the plane was a man and wife. She was in the center; he was on the outside, passed out, with eight or ten drinks inside him.

I sat there waiting for the question, and it got to be one o'clock, two o'clock, and we were due in London at five in the morning. At about three o'clock, the woman turned to me and said, "You don't drink or smoke, do you?"

I said no.

"Why?"

We barely had time to cover it, but I began to tell her about Jesus.

She said, "I wish I knew Jesus as well as you do."

"You can," I said, "right now."

Just then a waiter came through and almost dumped a tray of booze on us. We had to duck, and it kind of interfered with the proceedings. The woman said, "Well, this is not really the time, but when I get to the hotel, I'm going to ask Him to take over my life."

We happened to be staying at the same hotel, and when I saw her the next day, she was aglow with the glory of God.

One day a Jehovah's Witness came to my door, and under the power of the Holy Spirit, I welcomed him, and invited him in. In the natural, I didn't want to have anything to do with him. My human mind said, "This guy is a kook."

But the Spirit said, *Ask him in. Am I not able to save him?*

And I said, "Lord, I guess so. You saved me."

I hadn't really considered that Jehovah's Witnesses were candidates for salvation. I had built up sort of a doctrine in my head that that group was outside the pale.

"Come in," I said. "I'm glad to see you." That was Jesus glad to see him, not me. He came in and sat down, and I said, "You're one of many who have knocked on my door recently."

"Yes," he said. "We think the time is short, and we're doing our best to make converts."

"What is that in your hand?" I asked him. "A new Bible?"

He said, "No, that's a handbook of our faith."

"Well, could I see it?"

He seemed very pleased that I was interested enough to take a look at his handbook. The Lord was leading—I would never have thought of this. I would have said, "Get rid of the bum as fast as possible. I'm superior." But the Lord reminded me that I was brought from the position of a gutter bum by Jesus, and if He could bring me out of the muck of this world, He could do it for this boy.

I leafed through the book, and I found that Jesus Christ was a prophet, a good teacher, and that He was dead like everyone else. Well, that established his doctrine—he had no living Savior. So I said, "Where are you going to spend eternity?"

"Probably in hell."

"Well, then," I said, "why are you working so hard to bring others with you?"

He hadn't really thought about it. I hadn't either. It was the Holy Ghost beginning the session.

"How many of your group are going to heaven?" I asked him.

60

"Only a hundred and forty-four thousand. And the quota's all filled."

I could tell that he was not too well informed about *Watchtower* doctrine, so I pressed my advantage. "Well, then," I said, "why do you want to drag me where you're going?"

"Well," he said, "that's the way they've taught us."

Next, I opened the handbook under the heading of healing. It said, in black and white, that God used to heal supernaturally, but that He no longer does since doctors and medicine came on the scene. So I said to this boy, "Jimmy, it says here that God no longer heals."

And he said, "That's right."

I said, "Was this book written by authorities of your denomination?"

"Oh yes," he said, "it was."

"Has it been checked and double-checked and proofread by your authorities?"

"Very carefully so," he assured me. "It's all authentic."

I said, "Then you had better fire the printer. Because he put an untruth in this book. It says that Jesus no longer heals, that He's a dead prophet, but I know He's alive, because He healed me."

Jimmy turned white. He had to call me a liar or admit that his denomination was in error. He made a big mistake. He said, "Oh? Tell me about it."

And I told him how I simply read in the Bible that God heals, and I believed it, and I went up in the healing line in Oral Roberts' tent in 1954 in Baltimore and I received instant healing of a disintegrated spinal disk. Recent X rays showed no sign of damage to the disk.

Well, he was visibly shaken. He didn't know what to say. He couldn't call me a nut, because I was obviously healed. And he couldn't say that his handbook was wrong, so he said, "I'll tell you what. I'm a little bit new at this business. I wish you could talk to some of our older members— Would you go to church with me?"

"When do we go?" I asked.

That almost knocked him over, that I would go to his church with him.

I went to the Kingdom Hall the next Sunday. When they began to teach error, I tuned them out and began to pray in the Spirit. If you listen to a lie, you receive the spirit of the lie, and you receive deception. Being a Spirit-filled Christian, I could turn off my hearing and turn on Jesus good and strong. He made the words of error go right on by, so I wasn't deceived.

After we left the Kingdom Hall that day, Jimmy said, "How'd you like it?"

"I appreciate your interest in taking me," I told him. "By the way, how about coming to church with me tonight?"

He couldn't gracefully refuse, because I had gone with him. And he said, "I—er—a—all right."

He went with me that night, and he heard the word preached in power. He had already heard my testimony, and as Revelation 12:11 says, "By the blood of the Lamb and by the word of our testimony, we clobber the enemy." The Jehovah's Witness got saved.

Is anything too hard for God? Not when we live like King's kids and let Him give us the right equipment to do the job.

13
How to Find the Missing Day

One night, after I had found out that the Baptism in the Holy Spirit had really given me new power to witness, my pastor received a prophecy for me. It said that God would open doors for witnessing that I could not imagine. I was willing enough for that to happen, but I had no idea how it would come about. If I had tried to guess, I'd have missed it a mile.

The beginnings were way back in the sixties, when NASA began to function to carry out the President's directive to land a man on the moon. The program got in gear at Goddard Space Flight Center at Greenbelt, Maryland, not far from where I live. I was involved from the start, through contractual arrangements with my company.

Over the years, throughout the Mercury/Gemini series of space missions, I visited the tracking station in Bermuda in a consulting capacity. My notebook soon became filled with much interesting data which I frequently shared when speaking to high school and college groups on my favorite subject, "Science, Philosophy, Evolution, and the Bible."*

One of the stories I told often had to do with a part of the necessary ahead-of-time statistical preparation for the moon walk. The space scientists were checking the position of the sun, moon, and planets out in space, calculating where they would be 100 and 1,000 years from now. In addition, they were looking into the trajectories of known asteroids and meteors so we wouldn't send astronauts and satellites up only to have them bump into something. Satellite orbits have to be laid out in terms of where the heavenly bodies will be so that the whole thing won't become a head-on traffic collision.

Well, as they ran the computer measurement back and forth over the centuries, it came to a halt. The computer stopped and put up a red flag, which meant that there was something wrong either with the information fed into the computer or with the results as compared to the standards. They called in the service department to check it out.

"Nothing's wrong with the computer," the technicians said. "It's operating perfectly. What makes you think something's wrong?"

"Well, the computer shows there's a day missing somewhere in elapsed time," the operators said. They rechecked

*For anyone interested in reading about that subject, I recommend Dr. Henry Morris' book, *The Bible and Modern Science*, an inexpensive paperback available from the Moody Press, 820 North LaSalle Street, Chicago, Ill., 60610. To keep up with the latest discoveries in the age-old synchronization of scientific truth with the truth of the Manufacturer's Handbook, subscribe to the *Bible-Science Newsletter,* Box 1016, Caldwell, Idaho, 83605.

their data and scratched their Educated Idiot Boxes. There was no answer, no logical explanation. They were at a baffled standstill.

Then one religious fellow on the team said, "You know, one time when I was in Sunday school, they talked about the day the sun stood still." He about got laughed out of the room, because nobody believed him, but they didn't have anything else to try, so they invited him to show them what he was talking about. He got a Bible and turned to the Book of Joshua where Joshua was called to battle against all the Kings of the Amorites, kind of a formidable array of enemies. In the account, they found a pretty ridiculous statement for anyone who has an ounce of common sense. They found the Lord saying to Joshua, "Fear them not, for I have delivered them into thine hand. There shall not a man of them stand before thee." The Bible went on to say that the Lord slew Joshua's enemies with a great slaughter, and they began to flee before Israel. And the Lord cast down great stones from heaven, and more of the enemy died from the hailstones than were slain by Joshua's troops. But there were some of the enemy left, and Joshua prayed for the sun and moon to stand still until the Israelites had finished avenging themselves upon their enemies.

"And the sun stood still, and the moon stayed, and hasted not to go down about a whole day."

"There," the Christian space man said. "There's your missing day. Go ahead and check it out."

Well, they checked the computers, went all the way back

to the time when Joshua defeated the kings, and found the explanation was close, but not close enough. The elapsed time in Joshua's day was only 23 hours and 20 minutes, not a whole day. There was still a discrepancy of forty minutes to be accounted for. Consulting the Bible record again, they found that it did not say that the sun had stood still for a whole day, but for "about (approximately) a whole day."

So they were still in trouble. Forty minutes become extremely significant when they are multiplied many times over in orbits. Then the religious fellow remembered somewhere else in the Bible where it said the sun went backward. Naturally, the other space men told him he was out of his mind, but once again, they had no real choice in the matter, so they went back to the Bible and read in II Kings, the twentieth chapter, how Hezekiah on his deathbed was visited by the prophet Isaiah, who told him that he was not going to die, but that God would heal him so he would be well enough to go to the temple in three days. Furthermore, God promised to give him fifteen more years of life on earth. That was such good news that Hezekiah couldn't believe it! He asked for a sign as proof that God's word was true.

"Do you want the sun to go ahead ten degrees?" Isaiah asked him.

"No," Hezekiah said. "It's too easy for the sun to go ahead ten degrees. It does that all the time. It goes ahead every day. But how about letting the shadow return *back-*

ward ten degrees? That'll be a new thing, and then I can believe."

And so Isaiah spoke to the Lord, and the Lord brought the shadow ten degrees backward. Ten degrees is exactly forty minutes!

Twenty-three hours and twenty minutes accounted for in Joshua's day, plus forty minutes accounted for in Hezekiah's day—there was the whole twenty-four hours, the missing day that the space scientists had to make allowance for in the logbook.

I had given this account a number of times in schools and in meetings where I had been invited to speak, using it as just one example of how science is proving that the preposterous things in the Bible are true. And one day it came to the attention of a woman, Mary Kathryn Bryan, who had a column in a newspaper in Spencer, Indiana. She received a written copy of my remarks about the missing day from some unidentified source. Someone had probably prepared it after hearing a tape of one of my talks or had taken notes at a lecture and written them up. No one knows where the written account originated, but that doesn't matter anyway. It was an accurate report, and Miss Bryan was intrigued by it. Unknown to me at the time, she ran it in her column.

Well, I didn't know anything about her newspaper in advance, but I soon found out. Various news services picked up the story and it appeared in *hundreds* of places. My mailbox began to overflow with letters from people who wanted to know more about the missing day. The letters came from just about every country in the world—and they still come.

It was impossible for me to write a personal reply to each one, so I prepared a form letter explaining that the missing day is well-documented in the early writings of many ancient civilizations. For further details, I referred them to a book called *Joshua's Long Day*, written by a Yale University professor Dr. C. A. Totten, way back in 1890. In the letter, I gave a brief testimony of what my life had been like before and after I met Jesus, and I encouraged my correspondents to try Him for themselves. With the letter, I enclosed a review of Totten's book and a tract entitled *Did the Sun Stand Still?**

Some of the people, I've never heard from again. Some have written—or telephoned—to tell me I'm a liar, and I've had an opportunity to practice forgiveness. Numerous others have let me know that they have been saved as the Holy Spirit ministered to them through His word of truth. Hallelujah! That's what my pastor's prophecy was about! God *had* opened doors for witnessing that I could not have imagined.

Somewhat later, I received a call from the secretary of a pagan periodical in the midwest asking how a mythical God could do such things. When I answered her with my

---

*Tract available from Book Fellowship, Box 164, North Syracuse, N.Y., 13212. Copy of the form letter and the review of Totten's book are included at end of this chapter.

testimony of a Living Savior, she hung up the phone with a loud bang. Later, someone sent me a clipping from the publication for which she works, saying I had admitted the whole thing was a hoax. Shortly thereafter, numerous religious magazines, some of them Christian, began repeating the false "retraction" and apologizing for their original participation in the rerun of the article. Not one of them ever checked with me as to the truth or error of the article as originally published.

For the record—the report is true, the retraction false. Conversions that have resulted from the Holy Spirit working through the original article, the letter, and the tract, have demonstrated the truth of the word of God—"By their fruits ye shall know them." God doesn't save people through false reports.

The whole sequence of events has demonstrated to me how prone even Christians are to believe a lie instead of the truth, how ready they are to fall into Satan's trap. But God's word is true though all men be liars.

And my inability to furnish documentation of the "Missing Day" incident in no way detracts from its authenticity. "God said it—I believe it—that settles it." But even though I choose to not believe it, God still said it, and that really *does* settle it.

Quite understandably, NASA has been hard put to reply to the deluge of letters they have received on the subject, copies of which many inquirers have sent to me. One NASA letter disclaims all knowledge of me. Another gives my home address for further information, while still another acknowledges my affiliation with their program. It must be rather a strain trying to please all the religious, political, scientific, and ethnic groups to which they are exposed. Pray for them!

At the start of my controversial role in this incident, when accusations of "liar" — "hoax" — "phony" — began to come my way, I tended to become defensive and a little put out at God. After all, He had placed me in this embarrassing position of being without defense or excuse. Once or twice, in fact, I was right on the verge of throwing a massive pity-party—martyr pills and all! How could they *dare* doubt my veracity, honesty, and integrity!

Then the Lord seemed to speak: *Hill, what good reputation are you worried about?*

"Forgive me, Lord," I said. "Without You I am a complete phony instead of a partial one. But Lord, Your reputation is at stake," I continued.

To which He replied, *Hasn't it always been? And that's where you come in as My witness. You have to tell it as it is, and depend on My Holy Spirit as the only convicting, saving power in the universe.*

So my entire reliance is on God as my witness that it is all true as reported. King's kids are reporters, not explainers. Hallelujah!

And King's kids can live like King's kids as long as they choose His way, and stand by it. God will always honor the word of our testimony with fruit. What is the fruit of Christians? Baby Christians! And we are empowered to tell it like it is.

TO: *All who have requested more "Missing Day" Details.* (Joshua
10:13; II Kings 20:11)

Please excuse this form-letter reply to your request for more details about the Missing Day. Nearly 5000 letters and calls make it
impossible to write each of you a personal letter. I did not write the
article in question but have spoken on numerous occasions on the
Harmony of the Bible and Science and assume it was adapted
from one of these presentations. The *Evening World* of Spencer,
Indiana, first published it, and permission to reprint should be ob-
tained from them. Since the incident first came to my attention . . .
I have misplaced details regarding names and places but will be
glad to forward them to you when they turn up. In the meantime,
I can only say that had I not considered the information to be relia-
ble, I would not have used it in the first place.

The early writings of many ancient civilizations contain documentation of a "long day," a "day of twice natural length," etc.
Such statements appear in historical lore of the Aztecs, Peruvians,
Chinese, Babylonians, etc. The eminent scientist, Professor C. A.
Totten of Yale University, through his discovery of a day missing
in solar time, substantiated by astronomical processes the details
as set forth in the Biblical account. From the detailed procedure
given in his book *Joshua's Long Day* (available from Destiny
Publishers, Merrimac, Mass., 01860), anyone skilled in the art
should be able to write his own computer program.

While it is gratifying to see the perfect harmony between the
Bible and the world of science, a Christian does not need to prove
God in terms of His physical universe; his understanding should be
founded on the solid foundation of "Thus saith the Lord." Prior to
my meeting God personally through His Son Jesus Christ about
sixteen years ago, my life was dreary, empty boredom, and religion was a dry, lifeless, pious absurdity as I went from one group

to another with no change in the deadly monotony of the dried-out "churchianity" of frustrated seekers after Reality. Successful on the outside, within me I had an awful anxious uncertainty, an empty uneasiness that no amount of activity or attainment could satisfy. Being the product of an extremely stupid educational system which teaches only how to make a living but leaves out altogether any training in how to live, I was poorly equipped to cope with the grim reality of life, the basis of which is wild and irrational without a Personal God. After nearly a half century of searching for completeness and fulfillment, I met a man who had discovered that God has a first Name and that Name is Jesus, and that if I would invite Him to do so, He would move in and take up residence within me. I did and He did, and now the former emptiness and restless anxiety have been replaced with an inner peace and security that even the most violent outer turmoil cannot disturb, and His abiding Presence is continuous Reality. I became born-again by the Spirit of God and received Eternal Life from His own Son. All that tormenting burden of inner guilt and remorse were completely washed away as by a mighty river, and I now have that wonderful peace that only comes through being right with God. Shortly after I met Jesus Christ as my Savior, He baptized me in His Holy Spirit, and life is now a continuous adventure in this new dimension where the Gifts of the Spirit produce amazing results in my everyday affairs, as promised in First Corinthians 12-14.

Of the many interesting things I have learned about religious folks since your letters began pouring in several months ago, the most amazing is the readiness of some Christians to be negatively influenced by scoffers. A few derisive remarks from a pagan scoffer appear to send many of you scurrying for theological cover! It ought to be just the reverse, if we are walking in the power of God's Spirit. We are warned that in these last days the world will be full of scoffers but our faith should be solidly anchored to the Word of God, the unshakable foundation of all born-again people of God. My God is very much alive and readily available to all who will call upon Him for answers to life. Try the Baltimore Experiment for sixty days by simply asking Jesus Christ each morning to take charge of your life and affairs for just this one day. Then, as evidence that you are trusting the New Manager to handle all the details, acknowledge and thank Him for *all* that happens, regardless of appearances. Everyone I have known who has tried this has been highly pleased with results. Dare to place your trust in God, and He promises to satisfy the desires of your heart.

God bless you,
Harold E. Hill

BOOK REPORT "LONG DAY OF JOSHUA" C. A. L. TOTTEN

The recent news event based on Harold Hill's messages relates how an IBM computer crew confirmed the story of Joshua 10:13 of his Long Day while checking backward on trajectories of known asteroids and meteors to insure safe passage for our astronauts. As this story is being verified, may I present a review of another book written in 1890 by C. A. L. Totten who computed the year, month, day and even the hour of this event including the sequel event, the 40 minute longer day of Hezekiah. . . .

This tremendous mathematical work was completed and written up in his book in 1890, years before the computer was even a dream. His fantastic calculations were based on counting lunations and moon eclipses. These figures show 3333 years elapsed between the Joshua's Long Day and his book in 1890, and 2555 years between Creation and this 23 1/3 hour slow-down. If we add 80 years to up-date from 1890 to 1970 we find his Creation date i:

5971 years. His figure of 3293 years from Creation to Hezekiah's 2/3 hour slow-down indicates 738 years separating these two events which completed the full 24 hour slow-down.

Mr. Totten's Foreword points up the most remarkable timing in these events as he writes, "Such precision in timing is inconceivable to the mind of man." We find in Joshua 10:11 how the Lord cast down great stones from heaven killing more of the enemy than did the swords of the Israelites. These stones or asteroids were started on their lethal mission perhaps 2555 years earlier at Creation, timed to strike the earth at the exact day and hour to kill only the enemy as they were being chased by the Israelites. While we were recently amazed in the return of our astronauts within 5 miles of target after one week shoot-off, it is hardly comparable to hitting a moving target by stones sent out 2555 years earlier.

While Mr. Totten suggests an intervening comet perhaps caused the slow day by cutting off actinic rays, I feel a more realistic theory is to examine the possibility of a huge meteor or asteroid plunging into the earth's mantle slowing it down about one revolution while the inner molten core continued to rotate and eventually pull the mantle back in speed. Mr. Totten recounted how Newton demonstrated how the earth could be suddenly slowed down without appreciable shock to people.

I have examined several maps of the Pacific Ocean which lend support to this theory. The October 1969 map in *National Geographic Magazine* shows a large sink area between Hawaii and the Philippines with long fracture lines in the ocean bottom radiating outward to the continents. The effect of such a crash would be maximum there at the equator on slowing the earth and would result in huge tidal waves which might help explain Dr. Northrup's studies on California's sand deposits. The size of the asteroid needed to slow down the earth one revolution could be calculated if mantle thickness were known and it could have been as large as Ceres—480 miles diameter. The August 1970 *National Geo-*

graphic notes this and Hermes asteroid which approached within 500,000 miles of the earth in 1937. A map in the September 1969 *Scientific American Magazine* describes the magnetic deviations which generally all point to this depressed area and reflect known magnetic reorientation on iron-bearing materials when subjected to impact blows.

The 40 minute slow-down at the sundial of Ahaz could very well be caused by a smaller asteroid impact as seen on the moon's surface during the TV showing of our moon walkers.

Mr. Totten deserves the highest commendation of our newer generation not only for his tremendous mathematical genius but for the finest description of the purpose of his work as he wrote, "As the study of prophecy was impressively recommended by the Saviour, we must study it, and do so until we understand it; but in no wise may we dare alter it in jot or tittle."

> V. L. Westberg — August 1970
> Sonoma, Cal. 95476

14
How to Pray Without Ceasing;
How to Tame Your Tongue

One of the first Scripture passages to which God alerted me as I began to live like a King's kid was I Thessalonians 5:16-18: "Rejoice evermore. Pray without ceasing. In every thing give thanks: for this is the will of God in Christ Jesus concerning you." If we want to stay in the center of God's will all the time, we can't stop rejoicing, we can't stop praying, we can't stop praising God, giving thanks to Him.

When I encountered this Scripture, it sounded good—and impossible. Before I even tried the rejoicing evermore and giving thanks in everything, I knew I couldn't pray without ceasing. I could pray for about two seconds, and then my mind would wander. I'd think of other things. I'd try to get my mind back on the track, and I'd fall asleep. "Well," I'd tell myself, "I can do it tomorrow morning instead of to-night." But in the morning, I'd fall asleep again. No matter how hard I tried, I simply could not pray without ceasing.

I complained to the Lord about it. "Lord," I said, "there's bound to be something here that does not appear on the surface. You say I should pray without ceasing, and I'm willing, but I'm just not capable of it. There must be some dimension of prayer I'm not familiar with, one that I know nothing about. Lord, can You show me how to pray without ceasing, so I can be obedient to Your word?"

Before I could even say, "Amen," suddenly I was praying a new kind of prayer, the kind spoken of in Mark 16:17: "And these signs shall follow them that believe . . . they shall speak with new tongues." It was just rolling out of me. I didn't have to think up what to say, what to pray about, because I was praying in a language I had never learned. And it was so easy to pray. The prayer kept going and going. And although I didn't know *what* I was saying, I knew it was right, because of how it made me feel inside—so close to God, so aware of His power and His love, in such communion with Him. I guess I prayed for half an hour without let-up, the longest and most effortless prayer of my life up to that time.

Jesus said, *Continue to praise Me. Don't ever stop, and I Myself will keep the prayer chain going down inside of you, down in the temple of the Holy Spirit, where your gizzard would be if you had one.*

And He has been true to His word. There are always rivers of living water flowing down inside me. I'm always praising Jesus, joining in a prayer of the Spirit that's going forth all the time, interceding perfectly when I don't even know what to pray for, because the Holy Spirit prays through me.

That kind of prayer bypasses the mind, and oh, does it burn Satan, because he can't wiretap it. He can't tell what you're up to. And you can't mess it up either with your intellect. It's God the Holy Spirit, creating prayer from our human spirits directly to God at the throne of grace. You don't have to say, *"If* it be Thy will," because any prayer in tongues, any prayer in the Spirit, is automatically guaranteed to be right in the center of God's perfect will.

Before I began to pray in the Spirit, one of my besetting sins was a very caustic tongue. Being so superior myself, I was a master at raking everybody else over the coals. It didn't matter where I was, I'd have something ugly to say about somebody. The uglier it was, the more likely I was to tell it.

There was no doubt I had the ugliest tongue in the whole Christian fellowship. It was mean. I had trained it to be mean when I was a pagan. I took delight in cutting people to pieces. I never used profanity, because I had a Christian mother, and she taught me that only stupid people use God's name in vain.

"Someday you might want to call on Him in earnest," she said, "and if you waste His time by calling His name in vain, He might think you're fooling when you're deadly serious." I guess I was about five years old when she told me that, and I never forgot it.

But I sharpened my tongue in sarcasm, and I could find your weak spot in a few seconds and drill holes in you so fast that you wouldn't know what hit you until you were left hanging, hopeless and helpless.

When I got saved, and joined the church, I was a menace to the congregation. I could tell you what was wrong with everybody, the preacher included. I bad-mouthed every Christian with my sarcasm. The harder I tried to clean up my talk, the worse I got, and the louder the Book of James preached at me: "No man can tame the tongue." I must have read that verse a hundred times, but I must not have understood it even once, because I just said, "Lord, I promise to try harder." It should have been plain—even to me—that trying harder wasn't the answer.

One night in a prayer group, I had spread a piece of gossip about one of the brethren. I knew it was wrong as soon as it was out of my mouth, but I wasn't fast enough to grab it and pull it back in. Everybody stared at me, horrified, and I wanted to crawl under the rug. I felt thoroughly condemned, and as if that wasn't enough, one of the sisters motioned me to one side, and said, "Brother, did you ever realize what your tongue is doing to the fellowship?"

Talk about misery—I had it. I said, "I sure have, Sister Bessie, and I'm going to work harder on it." She looked at me and walked away, shaking her head. She probably knew that I'd been working harder on it already for three or four months, and the harder I worked, the worse my mouth squirted poison. I could feel the burning taking place down inside me, like ulcers growing.

The Bible says, "The words of a talebearer are as wounds." And I knew the truth of that by how my stomach cringed every time I spewed out poison against somebody. I was experiencing in my own body that death and life are in the power of the tongue.

I knew my tongue was ministering death—to other people and to me—but how could I tame it? That was a real question in my mind when I went home that night, all fed-up with me and my big mouth.

I had been told all sorts of things about do-it-yourself methods for taming the tongue, most of which would have resulted in my tongue being chewed into hamburger in nothing flat. I had read, "If your right hand offends you, cut it off. If your right eye offends you, pluck it out." But I could have cut my body down to a sliver without curing myself of my tendency to bad-mouth other people.

Suddenly I saw how futile, how hopeless, all *my* efforts had been and always would be. The truth of "No man can tame the tongue" broke into my consciousness. God showed me clearly that I could chew my tongue up until there was nothing left of it, and it wouldn't be tamed, because the roots of an unruly tongue are in the heart.

Finally God was able to get through to me: *Hill, until you let Me do the taming, you'll keep on wasting your time.*

I was past ready, so I said, "Lord, then tame my tongue on Your conditions." Immediately, I found myself praying in tongues. And from then till now my mouth has been cleaned up to the degree that I pray without ceasing, that I pray in tongues all the time. A tongue that is praising God cannot be criticizing anybody.

So many Christians say, "Do I have to speak in tongues?"

"No," I tell them, "you don't have to. You can minister death as long as you can stand it. You don't have to do anything God's way. You can do it your own way, like you always have. You can be a mean, raunchy, ugly Christian instead of a loving, joyful, peace-ministering one. You've got a choice. Which will it be?"

I have found that how I use my tongue has everything to do with whether I live a victorious life as a Christian or another kind of life. Turning my tongue over to Jesus was an important step in my learning how to live like a King's kid.

"But why?" you say. "The tongue is such a little member." Yes, it is small, but like the rudder on a ship, it is the director of operations of your whole body, the whole mechanism, the whole personality. And its natural tendency in the untamed state is to destroy, because, as James says, "The tongue is an unruly evil, full of deadly poison." God says the perfect man is the one who offends not in word—who has his tongue under control. But only God can control it. And His word guarantees that when you're rejoicing, praising, and thanking Him, you are perfect in God's sight, a King's kid for sure: "If any man offend not in word, the same is a perfect man" (James 3:2).

The Manufacturer's Handbook says praying in tongues is a sign for unbelievers. I saw a perfect demonstration of that one day when I was in a group of Mennonites in Pittsburgh, Pennsylvania, having been invited for a weekend to share with them. On Saturday morning, about eighty of the local men were there, and after I had spoken, I put out a chair for prayer. One of the men was very much of a scoffer. He was present to make sure that I didn't contaminate the brethren.

When another man came and sat in the prayer chair, I laid hands on him and prayed for him in the Spirit, praying in tongues. When the prayer was over, the scoffer was blubbering like a baby, crying up a storm, slobbering all over his expensive blue serge suit.

"What ails you?" I asked.

"Well," he said, "I don't know if the man in the chair got anything, but God spoke to me when you prayed for him, because you were praying in High German. I'm a student of High German, and I doubt if even you know it, because it's a rare language."

I said, "I don't know any German, high, low or medium."

"Well," he said, "God spoke to me in perfect High German and said, *Who are you to scoff at any of My gifts?*" And that big blubbering man got saved, and the next day, I heard him praying for someone in a new language. He was really turned on.

The Spirit will always witness to Jesus.

My friend, Starr Dailey, the former convict who wrote *Love Can Open Prison Doors,* was asked to testify in Tokyo in a Christian church. His interpreter managed very well until Starr opened the Bible. Then Starr discovered that the interpreter could translate only secular English words into

Japanese. He could not translate Scripture. Things came to a halt, for a moment.

Then Starr said, "Lord, I know You didn't bring me all these thousands of miles for a five-minute introduction. If You can't do anything about this, that makes two of us. But if You can, Lord, please do something."

The Lord came to him with a word from the Scripture: "I am the Lord thy God that brought thee out of Egypt. Open thy mouth wide, and I'll fill it."

Starr opened his mouth, and out came thirty or forty minutes worth of message—and he didn't know one word he spoke. It was Japanese, for his Japanese congregation. Starr said, "I had never realized that God could use another foreign language. I thought tongues was just something that was secret."

The Bible calls it "tongues of men and of angels." Whatever the occasion needs—High German or modern Japanese—God can provide it.

Why does God do it this way? I don't know. That's not my business. God wants to bless, and He can bless me any way He wants to.

Forgive us, Lord, for ever thinking that our God would give us anything except the very best that heaven has. Forgive us for listening to Educated Idiots who have brainwashed us into thinking that Your wonderful gift of tongues is from Satan. And Lord, have mercy on those preachers and on those uninformed people and on those ignorant ones, Lord. Enlighten them, and convict them by Your Spirit as

You have us that our God deals in only the very best for His people. Lord Jesus, we thank You for increasing our trust and our faith in You.

We want everything that You recommend that we ought to have as Your people. We want to leave out nothing, regardless of what theologians have told us, that it's not for today or it's not for us, but that it was for those folks back then. Lord, we're glad it was for them also. And we're glad tongues is for Your people today to witness in power, to see the unsaved come into the kingdom, to see the scoffers broken down, to see the eggheads changed. Tune up our tongues into the dimension of praise and thanksgiving, that never again will we be heard complaining or finding fault, or gossiping, or backbiting. Lord, put a watch over our mouths. Bind our tongues from gossip and loose them for witnessing.

Pour out Your spirit upon us and manifest Your gifts through us. As on the Day of Pentecost, they all heard the people glorifying God, let us live for Your glory. Thank You, Jesus.

15
How to Be Ecstatically Happy in Traffic

Traffic. That was one of the major problem areas in my life, and it came up regularly between four-thirty and five-thirty every afternoon. I'd be driving home from my plant, which was located in the industrial section of Baltimore, in the same area with Bethlehem Steel, General Motors, and a few other little outfits like that. There'd be about forty thousand other people trying to get home at the same time through narrow roads that were made for one-way horse-and-buggy traffic.

Oh, how I used to hurt, driving in that late afternoon madness. I'd work all day and get along pretty well praising the Lord, and then I'd hit the late afternoon traffic. In fifteen minutes, I'd be utterly exhausted. I used to sit at a light braced for action, my motor racing, and my blood pressure along with it. I couldn't relax those thirty seconds waiting for the light to change, because somebody just might get ahead of me. I had to beat everybody away from the light, and leave them eating my exhaust. Every light I encountered was the very longest. I always vowed the timer was set wrong, and deep inside I suspected it was done by somebody's malicious intent to bug me.

I used to wish I had a long steel pole slung underneath my transmission. It would be connected to a pushbutton under the dash, and when somebody got in my way, somebody who wouldn't move and let me go first in traffic, I could mash the button. The pole would ram through the other guy's tank on the back end and out the radiator on the front end, and it would serve him right.

Then one day, I came across the Scripture that said, "Love your enemies, bless them that curse you, do good to them that hate you, and pray for them which despitefully use you, and persecute you." It came through to me as "Bless those who bug you," and I knew God was talking about my attitude when I was behind a steering wheel.

"But Lord," I said, "*everybody* in traffic bugs me."

All right, He said. *You're the one who said he was going to try all the rules in the Manufacturer's Handbook. So start to bless those who bug you in traffic.*

Well, it was hard to do, but I promised the Lord I'd try. First, I'd dispense with my imaginary weapon. Then, by His grace, I'd try blessing those who despitefully used me in traffic situations.

That would take a lot of blessing.

The first night I tried God's way in traffic, I spotted a fellow sitting on a side street in total gloom. He was hungry, he'd worked hard all day, and he knew there were ten thousand cars full of pagans that still had to zoom past the intersection before he could hope to get out.

When I stopped and motioned for him to come out ahead of me, it almost finished him off. His eyes bugged out, and temporarily, he even forgot how to drive his car. He had thought he wouldn't get to drive for about two hours, so he'd turned off his ignition and just given up.

Well, when he started his engine and drove out, the whole traffic pattern changed. I saw him let somebody else out. I could feel the spirit of the rush hour lift, and I got so blessed I could hardly stand it.

Now I have a ball in traffic. When I pull up to a stop light, I watch the strained character alongside of me doing what I used to do. He mashes the gas to make sure everything's ready, pollution enough to kill the neighborhood squirting out the back end. When the light changes, I purposely hold back and let him take off first. And when he does, he grins from ear to ear. He's excelled in something for the first time in a month maybe. Maybe he's accepted the fact that he's a total failure, and then I make him a success by holding back in traffic. I've made his day, and I can see him perk up and brighten up in the old heap.

I just can hear that fellow when he gets home. He walks in the house, and his wife wonders why he's happy for a change. She's used to seeing him come in grouchy, like I used to, torn to pieces. But today he has excelled.

"Mama, the old heap is not so bad after all. You should have seen me beat a brand-new Mercedes away from a stoplight tonight." Maybe he gives her an extra hug and takes her out to dinner for a change, and tips the waitress a little extra, and—who knows? A blessing set in motion by King's kids acting like King's kids goes on forever.

I get home relaxed, praising the Lord, interceding for everybody all over the place, and when I walk in, Mama knows that I've been behaving like a King's kid. And if I get home tired out, she knows I've gone back to my old kind of driving.

There's no area of our lives that God can't straighten out if we let Him do it His way.

16
How to Quit Smoking

Willpower. That's a good word in the worldly world, and people who have a lot of willpower are congratulated and envied right and left. I should have known that I didn't have any, or if I had any, it was out on strike, because my willpower had been worse than worthless when I tried to use it to stop drinking, to stop backbiting, to accomplish any cleaning up in any area of my life.

One of the big things I tried to use willpower on was my smoking habit. I was smoking two packs a day, ten cigars, and a pipe. And that's a lot of smoke.

I had no fellowship in my Baptist church in those days. They thought I was a kook. And so, for spiritual fellowship, I used to go to a little Pentecostal church on Saturday nights. It was run by old Brother John Douglas, a great old saint of God, in a former movie theater in Baltimore. The saints would gather at about seven o'clock, and at twelve-thirty or one in the morning, they'd terminate their service.

Everything was beautifully ordered, a perfectly conducted charismatic meeting. One would have a song, another would have a Psalm, a spiritual song, tongues, interpretation, or prophecy.

When I walked into that church, everybody knew that I had arrived. I could see them wrinkle their noses. And I could hear them saying, "Here comes Stinky Hill," because I was the only smoker in about five hundred brethren, and everyone could smell me a mile away. It bothered me a lot, especially when they sang that old Pentecostal hymn, "There'll Be No Smoking in My Father's House." Everybody would look right at me. It nearly drove me up the wall.

Naturally, I tried to take action. Satan used the spirit of pride to get me to try to straighten up on my own to impress the brethren. I worked on it for a solid year, and at the end of a year, I had gone from two packs a day up to three packs, from ten cigars to twelve, and I was smoking a pipe twice as often as before—all by my very own effort.

Now, I was born-again and Spirit-filled, but those Pentecostals couldn't even believe I was saved. They'd get one whiff of me and turn the other way.

My pride was mortally wounded. I went home and tried harder to lay off smoking—really applied all the force of my willpower—and smoked more than ever. I praise God, because if I had been able to quit, God would have been robbed of the glory. And then I could have said to other smokers, "Why don't you get rid of that stinky habit of yours and get good like me, the Pharisee?" But God didn't fall into the trap. He does everything just right.

When I prayed, I kept saying, "Lord, give me the power to quit smoking," but the power didn't come. Then one day I quit asking and just waited on the Lord. And as I waited and listened, He seemed to say, *Why do you want to quit?*

I really hadn't thought that through. "Well, I want to quit because—" I didn't want Him to know that my image, my religious, pure, Christian, gentlemanly image shouldn't smell like I smelled. But He knew it already. And so He answered His own question for me.

You want to quit to impress the brethren?

"I guess that's it, Lord."

No guessing about it. You know very well that's your reason.

"Well," I said, trying to make myself look a *little* better, "that's one reason. And besides, it's killing me." I was beginning to cough blood, and I couldn't walk up three steps without panting.

Oh, yes, of course it's killing you—and has been all along. But that's beside the point. Lots of people die of things that are killing them, and they think they enjoy doing it. That's no reason at all. Be absolutely honest with Me, Hill, and then we can do business.

I hung my head and said, "Okay, Lord," and He accepted my confession.

Tell me, how did you stop drinking? He asked me next. *Did I give you the power to do that on your own?*

"Oh, no. I surrendered, I gave up. I said, 'God, help me,'

and You did. You did it by Yourself. You took my desire for alcohol away."

Well, then, He said, *why don't you give up on this and let Me handle it? Be honest. Admit you don't want to quit. Admit you're hooked. Tell it like it is.*

And finally I did. I said, "Lord, I have no power or desire to quit smoking. I have no power to change my will. I have no tendency to break this habit. I am compelled to smoke. I enjoy smoking. I will enjoy every cancerous puff as long as You permit me to, Lord." And then I got *real* honest and said, "Lord, I'm not even sure I want You to interfere with this habit I've had since I was thirteen years old." I acknowledged that my own will was so bound up in it, I wasn't even free to make a choice. And I finished up by saying, "Furthermore, if You leave it up to me, God, I'll probably get up to ten packs a day, and it'll start coming out my ears. If that suits You, that suits me just fine."

I simply became a pauper in spirit. I had fought a losing battle until I was exhausted, and I simply gave up. I could feel the release. And although I didn't yet know the words of Zechariah 4:6 in the Manufacturer's Handbook, I was ready to see a demonstration of "Not by might, nor by willpower, but by my Spirit, saith the Lord."

A week later, Jesus took my cigarettes away, and with them, all desire to smoke. I began to experience something about what the Bible means when it says, "Verily I say unto you, whatsoever ye shall bind on earth shall be bound in heaven, and whatsoever ye shall loose on earth shall be loosed in heaven."

After Ed had introduced me to Jesus, he had told me, "Don't try to make yourself worthy. Come as you are. Turn whatever you are over to Jesus, and *He'll* remake you into what *He* wants you to be."

I've learned that one of the most important things to learn if we want to live like King's kids is to trust the King with every problem, every fault, every sin, every impossible thing in our lives. He—and He alone—can make us fit for His Kingdom. As long as we keep trying to do anything by our own willpower, keeping the glory for ourselves, we are doomed to stay in our own puny kingdom of wretchedness and defeat. But King's kids loose everything to the King, and He sets them free to enter the gates of His Kingdom of Heaven.

17
How to Minister Healing

After my own healing, I began to see God's healing power at work in the lives of other people.

One evening, Jimmy—a man I had met in AA—and I were led by the Lord to go to the home of another member of our AA group. She had returned home from Women's Hospital in Baltimore after her third cancer operation in two years. The doctors had decided there wasn't enough of her left to cut on without cutting out life itself, so they sent her home to die.

Her mother greeted us at the door, and we said, "We heard that Naomi was quite ill, and we stopped by to—uh—to see her and—uh—maybe talk to her a little bit." We didn't really know why we were there. This was our first assignment in healing, just a couple of stupid drunks that Jesus had set free and filled with His Spirit. We were playing it by ear.

Her mother didn't want to open the door. "There's not enough left of her for a pleasant visit," she said. "Naomi's in very poor condition. Her body is eaten away—she's down to seventy-eight pounds—and I think it would be better if you didn't see her. The doctors say she has maybe a week, that's all."

We explained that we were members of the same AA group as Naomi was, and we certainly couldn't do her any harm if she was all that bad. We promised not to stay long, and her mother finally opened the door and took us up to Naomi's bedroom. What was left of her looked like an orange peel spread out on the bed, she was so thin and wasted, and her skin had turned that final death color of cancer. Naomi was dying and she knew it. There wasn't any doubt about it. Death couldn't be many hours away.

We greeted Naomi and she greeted us, and after we had talked a little bit, the Lord began to put ideas into our heads.

"God has kept us sober in AA for several years now, hasn't He," we reminded her.

She said, "Yes, that's right."

And then Jimmy shared with her how God had just healed him of bichromate allergy, medically incurable. It was as if God had given him a new set of skin, impervious to chemicals. And I told her how He had replaced my disintegrated spinal disk with a perfect new one.

She heard our testimonies and said, "That's wonderful."

And I said, "If God would do that for us, don't you suppose He would heal you?" I was surprised at the words as they came out of my mouth, because it hadn't occurred to me that God could heal someone as sick as she was. Actually, they weren't my words. They were the word of knowledge coming right out of my mouth by the Holy Spirit.

"Well," she said, "I guess maybe He could. I'd never thought about it."

"Would you like for us to ask Him to?"

"Well, yes, that would be nice." Naomi didn't have enough energy for showing any enthusiasm.

I took one hand and Jimmy took the other, and her mother just stood there in total unbelief. Our unbelief just about matched hers at that moment. It dawned on me that we were going to ask Jesus to heal an impossible mess—

But the prayer finally came—with stammering lips. It wasn't very elaborate.

"Lord, something's set in to mess up this body real good. But we know You're able to heal and to make new that which is destroyed by Satan. Jesus, please heal Naomi. Thank You." Then we prayed a little while in tongues and said, "Amen." Naomi said, "Amen," too, and that was the end of it.

As we had prayed, however, I felt the gift of faith rise up inside of me, and all of a sudden I *knew* that God would heal her! It wasn't a matter of *hoping* that something would happen. It was unthinkable that it *wouldn't* happen. A miracle had to take place, because the gift of faith suddenly popped right up inside of me. No organ music, no bells, no ecclesiastical vestments, just two drunks praying for a third one with Jesus in full charge. Hallelujah!

Then we went home.

About three months later, I was at a meeting one night,

and I saw a woman across the room who looked vaguely familiar. "She looks like Naomi," I thought, "but Naomi's been dead and buried for several months."

The woman saw me staring at her, and she knew what I was thinking. She came over to where I was and she said, "Yes, I'm Naomi. God healed me."

It was the faith of Jesus that I had felt welling up inside me when we prayed. *His* gift of *His* faith. It was a demonstration of what Paul wrote in Galatians 2:20: "I am crucified with Christ: nevertheless I live; yet not I, but Christ liveth in me: and the life which I now live in the flesh *I live by the faith of the Son of God,* who loved me and gave himself for me."

Any King's kid can minister healing to other people when he knows his rights and privileges.

A young Methodist preacher down in North Carolina came to our Spiritual Life Retreat for a year or two and received the Baptism in the Holy Spirit. One night, when we were on our way to Asheville where I was to speak in his church, he said, "I don't understand why God hasn't given me gifts of healing."

I was talking to the Lord while Jerry was talking to me, and I asked Jesus, "Why haven't You given Jerry gifts of healing?"

And the Lord seemed to say, *Ask him if he has ever acted like it.*

"Brother Jerry, have you ever acted as if you had gifts of healing?"

He said, "No. I never thought of doing it." And I just let him think about that for a little.

While we were at the church that night, a message came that one of Jerry's parishioners at the Asheville hospital needed ministry, sort of the last rites, because she'd been in a coma for ten days. The family sent word that it would be nice if the pastor could stop by. And so on the way back to the Retreat, we stopped at the Asheville General Hospital.

I said, "I'll sit in the car and pray while you go up and do what you have to do."

While he was up there, I was praying in the car, and the glory sort of started to trickle in, so I knew something was taking place up in the hospital room. When Brother Jerry came out, he was hitting only about every fourth step. He was a changed preacher, a shouting Methodist.

"What happened?" I asked him. I didn't ask, *"Did* anything happen?" because I could see that something had.

"Well," he said, "I walked into the room, and this elderly woman in her eighties was ready to die, and she expected to. Everybody knew she would. They had the casket all picked out and everything. But I just walked over to her bed, laid my hands on her and said, 'Sister, in the name of Jesus Christ, be healed.' And she sat up in that bed with her eyes wide open and said, 'Hallelujah.' She'd been in a coma for ten days." He shook his head, still dumbfounded. "All I did was act like it, and I found the gifts of healing were right there."

We contain the power of God, the gifts of God. All we have to do is act like King's kids and put them into action.

Even us? Yes. God uses even us.

If you pray for someone, and they drop dead the next day, pray for the next one. Praise God. Act like King's kids, and you'll begin to feel like King's kids. And the more you feel like it, the more you'll act like it. It's regenerative. It's cumulative. It increases all the time, and finally you get the message, loud and clear: *we are King's kids*. The kingdom of God is within us, and we're going to manifest it without.

If you have religious tendencies, you may find your EIB twitching at the way your theology is being clobbered. In fact, if you're very quiet, you may hear these words bubbling up into your think tank: "But everyone doesn't have all the gifts of the Holy Spirit. To one is given blah-blah-gurgle-gurgle— Doesn't it say so in I Corinthians 12?"

No doubt you've been listening to Dr. Tinkling Brass, that great theologian from South Clavicle Cemetery, who teaches at great length on the gifts of the Spirit—out of utter ignorance, never having himself experienced the power hookup which makes them available.

I, too, made the mistake of listening to him for a while one day, when I was too new a Christian to know better. I had just been healed in the tent of Oral Roberts, and Dr. Brass spent nearly twenty minutes proving that God's healing is not for today.

After enough of his strangulation of the truth to tear down

all but the strongest of faith, I began to pray for seminarians everywhere.

Then I said, "Lord Jesus, *You* tell me who the gifts of the Holy Spirit are for."

For the needy, He replied, *available to whosoever will deliver them, either singly or in groups, to bring completeness where there is lack.*

"Then why all the hesitation on the part of King's kids to use them?" I asked.

One reason—P-R-I-D-E— He answered.

And that is the whole answer, that most subtle of the enemy's approaches—the pride of life.

"Suppose they die?" Satan whispers at the moment of need where you may be the only one available to minister the gifts of healing. "Your beautiful Christian image will be wiped out. Go very carefully. Let so-and-so do it—"

But I say to you, just dare to permit the indwelling King to take over in all His resurrection power and glory. Then, if they drop dead, you can say, "Thank You, Jesus. Your answer happened to be 'No,' that time. Let's go on to the next one."

Jesus plus one King's kid is a majority anywhere—anytime.

18
How to Block Healing

God's will for the health of King's kids is plainly stated in III John 2: "Beloved, I wish above all things that thou mayest prosper and be in health, even as thy soul prospereth."

But we don't always prosper, we're not always in health. Why? Are there some roadblocks of our own making?

I used to think that God wanted to heal everybody and that everybody wanted to be healed. But I was only half right. I found it out at my first CFO Camp.

Blair Reed and I had gone there together. We had both just been healed, saved, and baptized in the Spirit, and we were ready to minister healing to everyone. We could spot the needs a mile away.

Another car drove up about the same time that we did, and a man got out, opened the trunk, took out a folding wheelchair, unfolded it, went around to the other side of the car, opened the door, and lifted his wife out, setting her up in the wheelchair. My friend Blair and I could hardly wait to get to her. We did remember that Jesus asked permission before He healed people, and so we didn't just run over and begin at once to pray. We asked permission first.

"Sister, Jesus wants to heal you. Do you want to be healed."

I was in for the greatest shock of my life when she indignantly replied, "I certainly do not." The expression on our faces must have showed we didn't understand, because she proceeded to explain: "For thirty years, I waited on that husband of mine hand and foot. Now he's going to wait on me as long as I live. I like it this way. You keep your hands off of me!"

And so I began to learn that everyone does not want to be healed. A lot of people enjoy poor health. It's a good way to throw a pity party and have somebody else feel sorry for you if you're sick enough, enough of the time. You can let it be known that you're bearing your cross.

Jesus' question, "Would you be made whole?" is the key to the situation. Wholeness involves a lot more than mere physical healing. Wholeness has to do with the total person.

One day a woman came to a meeting in which I was involved. She came Monday night for prayer, and Tuesday night, and Wednesday night, and Thursday night, and she wasn't one bit better. She had arthritis like I'd never seen before. Every joint in her body was locked up. It made you hurt just to look at her.

About Thursday night, I said, "Lord, we must be praying amiss, because she's not getting any better. How come?"

The Lord showed me that sometimes I'm stupider than I am at other times. Every once in a while, I temporarily get the impression that I know how to pray. But God says in Romans 8, *You don't know how to pray or what to pray for,* and it puts me in my place. So I said, "Lord, forgive me," and I prayed in tongues, and I asked for a word of knowledge. And the word of knowledge came: *This is a broken relationship, not a physical ailment. It only looks like one.*

God always has more information about a person than you'll ever get hold of in the natural. So, when her friends carried her up to the altar again Friday night, we all gathered around her. We said, "Lord, we're going to let You do the praying tonight. We're going to pray in tongues and ask You to interpret to us how we should proceed for our sister's healing."

As we prayed, it was revealed to us that resentment had this woman bound. There was a broken relationship between her and her sister.

I said to her, "Whom do you resent?"

"Oh," she said. "I don't resent anybody. I love everybody in the whole world." It was plain that her ego wouldn't let her be honest even for a minute. So the Holy Spirit reworded the question to put the blame on the other person.

"Who has done you a terrible wrong?" I said. "What did your sister do that injured you?"

Well, that set her free to tell us all about the cross she had to bear. The venom poured out of her system, like snake poison. Without the gifts of the Spirit operating, we might have sympathized with her, and she'd have sympathized even more with herself, and gotten still worse. But God let us see the bitterness, and hatred, and resentment down inside. And it all came out.

"That hussy! She moved into the neighborhood, came to our church, and she wasn't half as good an organist as I am, but the pastor gave her the job."

I said, "I bet that burned you up, didn't it?"

The woman had withdrawn the hand of fellowship in the Spirit from the local group, and her body had responded by locking itself up. Her hand was so locked up, she couldn't move a single muscle in her arm.

"Sister, are you willing to forgive?"

"That hussy? No! Never!"

We went over some of the Scriptures with her, those having to do with the binding up of the physical through the binding up of the spiritual. And we talked about the forgiveness business in the Lord's prayer. After a while, the Holy Spirit began to convict. She saw the awfulness of her bitterness, her resentment, and the inevitability of the physical effect it had on her body. We explained to her that Jesus wanted her to prosper and be in good health, as her soul prospered. That meant that relationship had to be healed before she could be healed physically.

Softening a little, she said, "I'm sorry. I can't go to her. It's too big for me to handle. It's been eighteen years."

I said, "I don't blame you. I don't think I could go ask forgiveness either after all those years of nursing that hatred.

I know I couldn't make myself willing. But would you be willing to go if God would make you willing?"

As she stood there at the altar, her friends half holding her up, I saw the struggle going on inside her. The bitterness was so firmly established—she was sure it was the other person's fault. But finally she said, "Yes, if God could make me willing, I'd be willing. I'm willing to be made willing."

And in that hour, her hand started to open. The God-given willingness down in her spirit set her free. I didn't see the total healing. We weren't there long enough, but I know that by now she's completely free, because she became willing to go and be reconciled.

It doesn't matter how medically impossible a situation may look, if we are willing to let God take all the roadblocks in our souls out of the way, His power will manifest itself. Impatience can be a roadblock to healing, unforgiveness is another, unbelief is another, frequently encountered.

There was no roadblock of unbelief in one of the brethren back in Lancaster County, Pennsylvania, with whom I had been on several witnessing assignments. Brother Herman came home from church one afternoon with a bad headache. He went to the medicine closet to take a couple of aspirin, and then he lay down to take a nap. About thirty minutes later, he woke up with his insides on fire. Checking the medicine cabinet, he realized that instead of aspirin, he had taken two chloride of mercury tablets his daughter had for athlete's foot. They were meant for external use only—chloride of mercury is a deadly poison.

There were two things he could do. He could panic, or he could praise God and stand on His word.

Panic is for pagans, not for King's kids, and so Brother Herman said, "Lord, Your Word says, 'If they drink any deadly thing, it shall not hurt them.' So this is Your problem, not mine." He locked the bedroom door, got down on his knees beside the bed, and turned it over to Jesus.

"Jesus," he prayed, "if You do not intercede—if Your word is not true—then they're going to have to break the door down to get out the corpse. I'll be the corpse. It's Your problem."

He went back to bed and woke up a couple of hours later, no headache, no stomachache, completely healed.

These signs shall follow King's kids: "If they drink any deadly thing, it shall not hurt them."

In the beginning of my life as a new Christian, I had a tendency to believe that now that I was saved, one of God's people, I'd be impervious to trouble. I had heard messages which led me to believe that when you become a Christian, nothing troublesome ever happens anymore. But God never promised to *keep* His people out of trouble. He said, "I'll *deliver* you out of trouble."

You have to get *in* trouble to get delivered *out* of trouble. Now, you don't have to *try* to get in trouble. Just plain living automatically takes care of that, but walking in the Spirit guarantees us protection against the powers of darkness which are always out to gobble up pagan kids and King's kids alike.

Recently I was driving down a divided highway to a meeting. The dividing strip was maybe twenty feet wide. Suddenly, a car coming from the other direction, going about seventy, the same speed I was traveling, started to cross the strip. It was headed straight for me. A one-hundred-forty miles-per-hour impact was in the making with me in the middle of it. Mincemeat.

I was glad that I didn't have to wait to get into the high gear of praise and thanksgiving, because I wouldn't have had time. It all happened fast. Walking in the light has to do with all circuits being tuned up by praise and thanksgiving all the time—in every thing giving thanks for everything. I had been walking in the light all day. So I was thanking God and praying in the Spirit for the people in the other car all in the same breath, realizing it could be my last one. But I was singing the songs of Zion, knowing that King's kids don't have to graduate on Satan's terms.

The car hurtling at me was less than twenty yards away when suddenly it shot straight up in the air, and turned upside down. It was a convertible, the top was down, and people flew in all directions. Then the car crashed flat, right alongside me.

"Lord, do You want me to stop?" I asked Him then.

No. Don't stop. You intercede, was the message I got. In my rearview mirror, I could see other cars and trucks stopping. They wouldn't need my physical presence there. But

God needed me to be an intercessor. And so I kept on praying, praising God, praying in tongues. I was aware of raw power, rivers of living water, flowing from my innermost being direct to the throne of grace as I interceded in the Spirit.

19
How to Avoid Auto Accidents, Tornadoes Firebombs and Falling Rockets

Before I was half a mile down the road, I had God's assurance that He had taken care of everything, and I went on to my meeting satisfied. That was Friday. On Sunday morning, I had an invitation to speak at the Kent Island Methodist church near the place where the accident had occurred.

I shared my experience from the pulpit and said that if anyone present knew the outcome of the accident, I'd like to hear about it. I knew something good had taken place. Sure enough, three different people came to me at the door of the church after the service and said they were at the scene just a few minutes after the accident happened, because they lived close by. The car had blown a tire, going at high speed, and had gone completely out of control. The people in the convertible had fallen clear of the car, and every one of them had walked away from the accident! The car was demolished—but no person was injured. It was a miracle.

A car coming straight at you on a level road does not suddenly jump straight up in the air. From straightforward motion to vertical motion is impossible unless you hit something curved to change the course. And that's what happened in that accident. The car's course was changed when it hit a curved surface—the curved circle of light that prevented darkness from entering to annihilate a King's kid. There were millions of foot pounds of energy involved, but that's nothing for an angel of the Lord. Hallelujah! When we call upon the King, He works supernaturally to deliver us from trouble.

One of the most dramatic examples I ever saw of how the King delivers His kids out of trouble was the case of a Spirit-filled sister out in Kansas.

Sister Tarwater was a brand-new Christian. She had just been filled with the Holy Spirit and had received the positive assurance of the Scripture that if she would mix the word of God with faith, all things were possible. God had put it in her mind and in her heart and in her whole being, that no matter what happened, she was to stand on God's Word and watch for His deliverance.

Sister Tarwater was working in the kitchen one day when a tornado warning came over the radio. She looked out the window and saw the big, black twister coming slowly across the plains, gobbling up, tearing up, destroying everything in its path. Houses were flying, and cows and barns—total destruction. Her two children were playing out in the backyard right in the path of the thing. But instead of succumbing to fear, she said, "Lord, with God all things are possible, and You said to take authority over the powers of darkness, and that's what I'm going to do."

She went out on the back porch. By this time, the twister was within a couple of blocks of her house, coming straight toward her. She could almost see Satan sitting on top of that big old black thing, so she pointed up and said, "Satan, in the name of Jesus Christ, get that thing out of here," and as soon as she had said the words, the twister turned the corner and went down the side street, wrecking everything in its path. But on Sister Tarwater's house, not a shingle was touched. She had taken advantage of her privileges as a King's kid.

And God is glorified every time she tells about it.

If all things are of God, as God says in II Corinthians 5:18, nothing accidental happens to a Christian. Everything that happens can somehow glorify God if we dare to stand on that and dare to act like it in every situation. You'll get into some exciting spots. And God will get more glory than if you didn't.

I was in an exciting spot a couple of summers ago. I had an invitation to speak at a Full Gospel Business Men's meeting in Albuquerque, New Mexico. It was while the rioters were burning and bombing the city. They had taken over control suddenly, without too much warning, and they had Albuquerque well under control of their fire program.

117

My less fanatical friends at home tried to talk me out of going. They said, "You're certainly not going out there. That's a hot trouble spot."

I said, "Of course, I'm going. Where do you find Jesus but *in* trouble spots? That's what He came for. King's kids never back away. King's kids walk in and possess the land when God makes the way and gives the assurance. It's our responsibility as Christians to heal the sick, to cast out devils, to set the prisoners free. Isn't that what Jesus said? All right. Of course, I'm going."

It didn't take much faith on Saturday morning to get on an airplane in Baltimore; it took a little more to see the fires and still praise the Lord as we approached Albuquerque. There were about three million dollars worth of buildings in flames as we flew over the city, they told me afterward.

But I kept my mouth in action: "Praise You, Jesus. Praise You, Jesus. I don't feel like it, Lord, but I'm going to praise You anyhow." It's not a sacrifice of praise until you don't feel like it, is it? I kept on praising Him out loud.

The president of the local Full Gospel chapter met me at the airport, and that night we went to where the meeting was to take place. The manager greeted us at the door with, "I hope you folks are not planning to meet here tonight. The rioters have sent a personal message saying they will firebomb you and burn you out. They've been burning buildings on schedule in Albuquerque all week. You're next on the list. They do not like Full Gospel people."

He went on to say, "I've made contact with a local church,

and they'll be glad to let you use their facilities a couple of miles up the road. You might be safer there."

"Safer?" we said. "What do you mean safer? Can King's kids be any safer than on an assignment for their boss? Of course not. We're not running from Satan. We're not backing up one step. We're going to stand still and see the salvation of the Lord. We're King's kids, remember?"

Well, then he panicked. He pleaded. He begged. He practically threatened. He did everything. Finally he warned, "I can't be responsible for what happens to you people."

We said, "Who asked you to? Jesus is responsible for His kids when they're on His business."

"But," he said, "it's dangerous."

He didn't have to tell us. We could hear the fire trucks and the sirens all around us. The rioters were in business, in full production for destruction. And they were zeroing in on us as a prime target.

The manager was getting more shook up every minute, and we couldn't much blame him. But he let us in, and we had dinner. Some of the folks at the meeting looked a little nervous, and we couldn't blame them either.

We said, "Look. If there's anybody here who would rather be elsewhere—by all means, go right now if you'd feel more comfortable." We knew we couldn't afford to have a complainer or a fearful one in the group.

A few of the folks got up and left, and we had all oneness and one accord.

Outside, it was bedlam. The manager of the restaurant

pulled the curtains around—I guess he thought that would ward off some of the hotter bombs temporarily. And then we turned it over to Jesus. We said, "Lord, this is an opportunity to find out if Your Word is a lot of fairy tale Sunday school talk, or if You mean what You say." Tempting God? No, indeed. Just checking out His Word to see if it works, that's all. And we said, "Lord, if Your Word does not work, we're going to find out once and for all. We'll leave here very shortly with flaming shirttails as proof." We were beginning to get excited.

So we started our meeting, singing songs of victory. And the manager of the restaurant went from window to window all evening looking for the firebombers. Oh, we kept hearing the firetrucks and the police sirens all around us, but they didn't come nigh unto us, because— Well, I don't know how He handled it, whether God sent a legion of angels to catch the firebombs and blow them out as fast as they came, or what. But we didn't see one bomb.

That was not one of my shorter talks. I spoke for about two hours and fifteen minutes, and then we had some ministry. We broke up close to midnight and went home.

Now I can reliably report that God can deliver His kids from firebomb threats. I couldn't have done that before Albuquerque, one more example of how God will deliver out of trouble every time we praise Him.

Another day, God gave me another chance to know that King's kids can walk through the very valley of the shadow of death and fear no evil.

I was in the NASA space tracking station at Coopers Island in Bermuda. It's there that missiles are released to go into orbit if all systems are go, or brought down if things are malfunctioning.

That day, everything was functioning properly. The first-stage rocket disengaged, and began to fall, and the rest of the vehicle continued on upward. And then suddenly we saw that someone had goofed. They had set the computers a little bit slow, and the first-stage rocket was falling directly on top of us, some forty or more space scientists and one King's kid.

It was all electronically portrayed on the wall of the tracking station as we watched in horrified unbelief. The tremendous cylinder about the size of a couple of country barns end to end was coming straight down on top of us.

We saw it coming, but we couldn't do anything about it. The space station at Coopers Island is right out on a point of rocks with a steep drop of several hundred feet down into the Atlantic Ocean all around.

There was no place to run, and so I began to rejoice. I said, "Hallelujah, Lord! This looks like graduation day. In a few seconds I'm going to be with You. When that thing comes down, I'm going up. Hallelujah!" I wasn't afraid—I was joyful.

And then the Spirit checked me, and the Lord seemed to say, *What do you think I've got you here for? To rejoice in your own graduation? Start to intercede for these other people who are not in your enviable position.*

121

And so I began to pray in the Spirit. And as that perfect prayer went up, I saw a law of physics violated in front of my eyes, the law that says a free-falling body never changes its trajectory, never moves its path unless it is acted upon by external forces. In other words, it falls in a path that doesn't deviate unless there's a tremendous side wind or something like that, which there was not. It was a calm and quiet day except inside the tracking station. There it wasn't calm and quiet. There was panic among the eggheads, but I had the Comforter.

And as I prayed in the Spirit, it was as if a giant hand swept that first-stage rocket right off out of trajectory, disturbed its path by many degrees, and it splashed a few hundred yards from where we were sitting, right out in the Atlantic Ocean.

God delivered us from certain destruction that day. But even before the deliverance came, I knew only joy. I knew what the psalmist knew. "I will fear no evil—even in the midst of the valley of the shadow of death."

When we praise God and pray in the Spirit without ceasing, He changes His permissive will to His perfect will right in the middle of what's going on. His permissive will was that forty or so of us were dead that day. His perfect will said, *No. Wait until more of these men are saved.* King's kids have a lot to do with the postponing of circumstances that are about to happen to themselves or others.

Begin to act as if the promises of God might be true. Walk into the situation. "Lord, You said it. If it doesn't work, and

You can't make it work, then that makes two of us, because I certainly can't. But I'm going to find out if You can. Let the firebombs come. Let the enemy do his best or his worst."

Stand and see the salvation of the Lord. This is acting like King's kids.

Then the world of darkness will come around and say, "What have you got? I believe I need that."

And when they ask a question, they're entitled to an answer: "It's Jesus. He has me. I have Him. That makes me a King's kid. Hallelujah!"

20
How to Praise God For Car Trouble
How to Sidestep Lawsuits

Praising God in the midst of everything that happens can lead King's kids into some highly interesting chains of circumstances. Over and over again He has taught me that He will work all things together for good if we love Him, trust Him, and are obedient to praise Him and thank Him for everything.

One sunny Saturday afternoon, three of us King's kids were driving into Harrisburg, Pennsylvania, to a Full Gospel meeting. I was driving a car with a floor shift, and somehow, pulling away from a stop, I got it in reverse instead of in second gear, and the shift handle came right out of the floor. It hung from my hand about as useful as a wilted stalk of celery. There was no way to shift gears, and I was blocking all kinds of traffic.

Horns were blasting at us from every direction. There was enough horn power to move us across the street, practically. But it didn't. We just sat there.

The natural thing was to tell the brethren to get a taxi and go down to the meeting while I tried to get somebody to fix the car. But we tried the *super*natural thing instead.

I turned to Bud and Bob, the two brothers with me, and said, "Let's find out how God can deliver us out of this mess if we praise Him in the midst of it." They nodded their agreement.

One of them said, "I don't know of a better place to try it." And the three of us began to praise God.

"Hallelujah, Lord. We're in trouble. How are You going to get us out of it?"

Outsiders looking on might have said, "You're out of your mind. Why don't you get out and push?" But we weren't listening to outsiders. God's instructions to King's kids are, "Praise Me. I will deliver you." And so we didn't get out and push—we praised.

While we praised, I took the gearshift handle and poked it down in the hole, and it caught first gear at a roaring six miles an hour or so, enough for us to creep out of the way of the truck traffic and into a service-station yard. When the attendant had heard our plight, he shook his head.

"You're in bad shape today—Saturday afternoon. Mercedes, foreign car, out-of-state license. You'll probably have to wait until Monday." He offered to let us leave the car with him.

"No thanks, we'll travel on to our meeting," we said. He raised his eyebrows and pointed toward downtown

126

Harrisburg where the convention was being held—two or three miles away—and shook his head again.

Well, we started down the road praising the Lord. "Thank You, Jesus. This is a mess, but it's raw material for Your glory. We're going to keep on praising You."

Psalm 50 says, "Offer unto God thanksgiving; and pay thy vows unto the most high." David's vow was, "I'll praise You with every breath." That sets you up to enter into the next verse: "And call upon me in the day of trouble: I will deliver thee, and thou shalt glorify me."

As we crept along on a side street, waiting for Him to deliver us, suddenly, over to the right, I saw a sign: MERCEDES BENZ SERVICE. Hallelujah! We were in business. I drove in confidently—but the place was locked up tight.

We kept praising the Lord, anyhow, wondering, "Lord, what's next?" We prayed in tongues, and we prayed in English. We prayed expectantly, "Thank You, Jesus. Thank You for what You're going to do. We don't know how You're going to do it, but we know You're going to take advantage of this trouble to bring glory to Your name. You're going to deliver us because You promised. You're going to take this mess and make a message out of it. Thank You, Lord."

The next thing we knew, a man from the service station next door came out and asked, "You in trouble?"

"In a way," I told him.

"Well," he said, "the Mercedes service manager was

here this morning, but he had no mechanics on duty, and it's such a nice day, they decided to close up early. They're gone for the weekend."

I said, "Well, I see they're closed, all right. Praise the Lord." He looked kind of puzzled, and so I explained, "We're praising the Lord, anyhow. We're not going to stop."

That got him a little bit worried about what kind of people we were, so he volunteered, "I have the manager's home telephone number—"

"You do?" I said. "Well, praise the Lord."

"In fact, I'll get him on the phone for you." With that, I could see him begin to do our worrying for us. Somebody has to worry. And if King's kids refuse, somebody else will always do it for them.

He got the service manager on the phone, and turned the phone over to me. I hadn't done anything yet except praise the Lord, and my two kooky friends were still in the car praising the Lord.

When I explained our trouble to the service manager, he told me what I already knew.

"Well, I'm sorry, but we're closed today, and I don't have any mechanics I can call." It sounded final. The last word.

I said, "I understand. It's all right. Praise the Lord." I didn't try to talk him into anything, but the next thing I knew, he was saying, "Tell you what. Wait just a minute. I'll be right down."

Well, I thanked him and praised the Lord some more. I knew that service managers do not perform service functions. They don't work with tools—they've graduated to a higher level—management. But this service manager seemed to have forgotten that. He drove in a few minutes later and got out of his own Mercedes without saying a word. He didn't look at me, he didn't look at anybody, he just got in my car with a little handful of tools and sat there for a couple of minutes. I don't know whether he was praying or not. He looked like he might have been.

I saw the service manager take the gearshift handle, kind of wobble and wiggle it around in the hole in the floor, and all of a sudden he looked kind of happy, like he was onto something. He held the gearshift in place with one hand and bammed it with the other hand. It meshed right down into the right place among all those gears. A thousand to one. Next, he shifted all the gears, drove the car around the block, came back and said, "That's all. All fixed." It had taken him five minutes.

"How much do we owe you?"

"Nothing."

I had to force him to accept some money for taking his own personal time, leaving his house, and coming down to fix a car for a King's kid. (Glory to Jesus—I had prayed for a fresh word of testimony for the meeting that night. Now, I had it!)

Well, I thought that would be the end of it. But it was only the beginning.

Early one morning the next week when I was praising the Lord and thanking Him for His goodness to me, He reminded me, *You were pretty grateful for that service you got up there in Harrisburg, weren't you?*

"I sure was, Lord."

Well, why don't you write and tell them about it?

I had never thought of doing that, but it seemed a good idea, so I sat down at the typewriter and wrote a letter to the service manager of the Mercedes Corporation at Stuttgart, Germany. I explained how three of us Christians had been on our way to a Full Gospel Business Men's convention and car trouble had developed and we had praised God for it and prayed in the Spirit and the Mercedes manager had taken his own time to come down and fix it and had refused pay for it. I told him that was the very finest kind of service I had ever had from any man anywhere, and that as far as I was concerned, I would never drive anything but a Mercedes as long as I lived if I could afford it.

I just told it like it was. Then I addressed an envelope, licked some stamps, and sent the letter on its way to Germany.

Right away, Satan began to accuse me: "Hill, you're ridiculous! You're out of your mind. You don't write to officials in Germany in that kind of language."

But I said, "I do, because I'm a King's kid, and I'm free to use any kind of language I want to. I'm free to tell it like it is. I don't have to care what anybody thinks. The results are not my business."

Well, three months went by, and Satan got me to agreeing with him. "Yeah, that was too hot for them to handle, all right. They just didn't know what to do with that one."

And then one day a letter came back from the Director of Services for the whole Mercedes Corporation. He said, "We were so grateful for your letter. People hardly ever tell us the good things. In fact, it was such a nice letter that we had copies made and sent them to all of our service areas all around the world, holding up Harrisburg as a prime example of how a service agency ought to be run." He went on to say that they were sending me some further information about their company. They couldn't do enough for me.

Talk about a testimony! But that still wasn't the end. There was more. There's never an end to a word of testimony that starts with an attitude of gratitude. If day and night you will delight in the laws of the Lord and meditate on them all the time, blessing will be automatic. Whatever you do will prosper. Chaos will turn into order. Disorder will turn into order, because God orders the atoms of every situation to behave like they ought to for King's kids.

And so, a few weeks later, I got another letter from Stuttgart. This one was signed by a woman, the personal secretary of the Director of Services for Mercedes Benz. She wrote, "I read your letter, and I have never read another letter like it. Where did you get the faith to depend on God for such things? I'd like to know more about that kind of faith."

I could tell that she was crying out for reality. "How can

131

I know God like that?" she asked. Well, she had asked a good question, and she was entitled to a good answer.

God had already set it up for her. Just a year or so earlier, I had been in Germany and had spoken at an International Christian Leadership Conference in Wiesbaden. In my talk, I had mentioned the power hookup with the Head Man of the universe via the Baptism in the Holy Spirit. The German woman who had interpreted for me was secretary for the ICLC for West Germany. She was already a born-again Christian, and when Jesus was lifted up as Baptizer, she began to thirst for the rivers of living water.

She said, "You know, I've suspected for some time that there's more to Christianity than what I have experienced." She had been to Washington and had heard Catherine Marshall speak at a prayer group. When my talk was finished, she said, "I want to hear more about Jesus, the Baptizer."

There was no prayer room set up in the hotel, so we had gone to a corner of the dining room, and while the waitresses were setting the tables for a luncheon, we had a Baptismal ceremony. Jesus will baptize anywhere.

As a result of that service, I had the address of a German Spirit-filled Christian to send to the Mercedes secretary at Stuttgart. "There just happens to be a Christian woman who lives right down the Rhine River from you, in in the town of Ulm, who will be glad to tell you all the details of the faith," I wrote.

And so, on account of a torn-up gearshift transmission in Harrisburg, Pennsylvania, a woman in Germany got saved, born again, and filled with the Spirit. Farfetched? Nothing is farfetched with our God, because He is the beginning and the end, and He knows the start and the finish and all the in-between.

Now, if I'd used my common sense when I had my car trouble, none of this would have happened. Common sense would have settled for griping and complaining, for having the car repaired on Monday when the regular mechanics came back to work. But King's kids don't have to settle for common sense like pagans do. King's kids can praise God in everything, and have *un*common sense, divine sense, revelation sense, working for them—overtime.

How far can we go in trusting Jesus? How far can the King go in meeting the needs of King's kids? Just as far as we'll trust Him and be obedient to His word. The impossible is His specialty.

A while ago, I submitted a contract on a large government project. On that particular project, I was so sure that I was thoroughly familiar with all the details that I didn't bother to read the fine print. And I signed the contract and committed our companies for everything we owned, because when the president signs the paper, that's it.

Later, I read the fine print, and I found we were in serious trouble. It required us to do something which was impossible for us to do. And the out-of-town contractor sent us registered letters to put us on notice that the next communication we received would be the institution of a lawsuit for everything we owned. The government was involved, the army engineers, seven contractors, hundreds of people— Top priority. Penalties on top of penalties— There was no way to undo what I had done.

I don't mind telling you, I panicked. I said, "Lord, what'll I do now."

Well, it seemed like He said, *It's a little bit late to ask that question. You didn't ask Me before you signed the contract.* You see, I goofed. Don't get the idea that I do these things perfectly, but I know what to do about it when I goof. I know my rights and privileges as a child of the King. I know that my Heavenly Father has provided all kinds of latitude for His kids to goof, and then what we do about it is what determines the outcome.

I couldn't cover it up and say, "Well, it wasn't really that bad." And it hurt my pride that I had done something that the lowest paid clerk in the outfit wouldn't do— signed a contract without reading the fine print.

I was tormented day and night, about to lose everything that I had worked for all of my life, and I couldn't even pray. Satan was injecting continual torment: "You're going to be a pauper. You'll have no roof over your head." And I wouldn't. He was right. And I don't even own a tent. I was going to have to go and borrow a tent from somebody to live in. Now this was stark reality, right in the business where I'm supposed to be the top executive. It was very rough on the pride.

What does God say to do? If we confess our sins, He is faithful and just to forgive us our sins and to cleanse us from all unrighteousness.

"Lord, I have goofed. I have really made a boo-boo. How are You going to get us out of this mess? Hallelujah!"

The commonsense thing was to stay at home and sweat it out and become a total nervous wreck. But I left the impossible situation in God's hands, and headed for a retreat in North Carolina.

At the retreat that night, the Lord said, *Confess your faults one to another.* So I stood up before the meeting to tell them what I'd done. I didn't like to do that. It ruined my image. But if I didn't get it out of the way, it was going to ruin *me*, not just my image.

Satan had all of his tormentors going in both ears: "You've really done it. You'll never get out from under this one. You might as well give up."

I said, "God's kids never give up. Praise God. We don't know how our God's going to get us out of it, but He's promised to do it. He said in Psalm 50: 'Offer unto God thanksgiving and pay thy vows unto the most high and call on me in the day of trouble, I will deliver you and you shall glorify me.'"

I said, "Lord, I'll be glad to give You the glory, because no man can deliver me."

And so I stated the situation in a few words. And I said, "Brethren, I can't even pray. Pray for me." They gathered around, laid hands on me. I praise God for the brethren. We need the fellowship. If I hadn't had them, I would have gone out of my mind with torment. It's one thing to tell you how to do it, but it's another thing to be in the middle of it yourself. And I was in the middle of it then. I'd been dishing out a lot of advice about how to get out of such messes, but I'd never been in one. I had been telling people how to come back from where I'd never been.

And so they prayed for me in tongues, and the interpretation of the prayer was beyond anything I'd have had the nerve to pray with my understanding:

"Lord, make this whole transaction as though it had never existed."

It was a ridiculously impossible prayer, but it had been prayed. No way to call it back. And so I waited, day after day, for the lawsuit for our breach of contract to begin. Every day Satan kept needling me, "It'll come tomorrow." But tomorrow it didn't, and days passed, weeks, and finally years without any further mention of lawsuit. During that time, I had to learn to praise Jesus all the time or else fall in the hands of the tormentor.

I don't know what happened. That contractor still has my signature on the paper. And he is entitled to hundreds of thousands of dollars damages unless God changed the minds of many people. I can't explain to you how it happened. I'm just reporting. God is in charge. He used to be my partner, but no more. Since I've started to live like a King's kid, He's Head Man. Hallelujah!

21
How to Fly Through a Fog
How to Get a Perfect Preacher
How to Build a Foolproof Bomb Shelter

Over and over again I see how God gets the world to
treat us like King's kids if we follow His instructions for
Kingdom living, giving thanks for everything, praising
Him for what pleases us—and for what doesn't please us—
because He says, *Give thanks for everything, for this is
My will for you.* Whatever old Slue Foot means for harm,
God can use for good—if we're acting like King's kids.

One day I was scheduled to speak on TV at Greenville,
South Carolina, for a Full Gospel Business Men's program
at seven-thirty in the evening. I went to Washington,
D.C., to catch my plane at two o'clock, expecting to
change planes at Charlotte. Well, my plane didn't take
off at two o'clock. It couldn't. It hadn't even arrived in
D.C. yet; it was lost out in the fog somewhere.

The natural tendency was to panic, to get all disturbed,

but I said, "Lord, I'm praising You. I haven't had a chance just to sit down quietly and study the Word uninterruptedly in I don't know how long." So I sat in the D.C. airport and studied, and the fog got thicker.

I telephoned the secretary of the chapter at Greenville and said, "I'm going to be late. I don't know how late."

"Well," he said, "praise the Lord."

I said, "That's the best thing I've heard all afternoon. I've heard all kinds of griping and complaining around the airport." You never heard anything like it. There must have been two hundred gripers—and one praiser. I was glad to have another praiser at the other end of the line. It gave me courage to continue to praise. We agreed over the phone that God's perfect will was being served. Now we couldn't understand how it could be served by my not even showing up maybe, but that was God's problem.

I said, "Lord, it's all the same to me whether I go to Greenville or drive back to Baltimore." I released it to Him. I loosed the whole thing. What you loose on earth is loosed in heaven.

Next thing I knew, the plane had arrived. We made it into Charlotte, but when I stepped off the plane, I was surprised. The fog was so thick that a duck wouldn't have flown that night out of Charlotte. Still, I was being paged as I came into the airport. The airline's employee asked, "You're scheduled to go to Greenville?" When I said yes, she explained that they had hired an air taxi—a private plane—to take me down.

How to Fly Through a Fog
How to Get a Perfect Preacher
How to Build a Foolproof Bomb Shelter

Well, praise the Lord for special arrangements for King's kids. I'd never had that happen before—but when I looked out, I couldn't see the field, much less the air taxi. But I kept praising the Lord. When you're walking in the light, you don't have to see it. If it's foggy, you just believe it.

The pilot looked like he didn't care whether it was sunlight or dark. It was just another flying job to him. I heard the airline tower ask him how long it would take. He said, "Forty minutes from the time I leave the ground." And for forty minutes we saw nothing but swirling fog.

Below us, somewhere, were high-power lines and mountains, but we flew blind until we saw the airport's flashing lights when we were about twenty feet from the ground. The secretary was at the airport to meet me, and it was five after seven.

He said, "If we can find the mountain, we'll go up to the TV station. It's fogged in, too." But he had made a trial run the day before and thought he could find the mountain, at least.

Well, we found it and followed the white line to the top of the mountain and walked into the studio at seven twenty-nine, with one minute to spare. But the group up there had been sweating out that close timing. So they had switched hours, letting Dr. Bob Jones, president of Bob Jones University, go on at 7:30, rescheduling me for eight o'clock.

Why, I couldn't have bought that spot for one million

dollars. But God put me on that hour. I told the whole listening audience about the gifts of the Holy Spirit, that tongues are for today and healing and all the other gifts of the Spirit. Now, was God in charge of proceedings? Is there anything too hard for God?

Sometimes people ask me, "You mean you're still a Southern Baptist?"

"Of course," I tell them. "But I'm no longer a standard-brand Baptist. I've been tampered with—Hallelujah!"

I freely confess that many times during those early years when rejection and criticism were my sorry diet, I wanted to leave those "heretics" and join the Pentecostals where I was appreciated. In fact, hardly a day passed without my organizing at least one pity party around a platter of martyr pills.

But the Lord seemed to say, *Why do you suppose I've hooked you up, Hill—to run away and deprive others of My blessings?*

Many a time my, "Okay, Lord," was weak and sickly, because I simply did not appreciate being unappreciated.

Time after time, when I felt rebellious, the Lord would read my thoughts and again give the directive, *Stay where you are and tamper.*

One night, as I was criticizing the church instead of fulfilling my role as intercessor, the Lord nearly spoke aloud and said, *If you do not like your church, pastor, or brethren, it's your own fault. Stop being part of the problem and start being instrumental in bringing about the answer.*

How to Fly Through a Fog
How to Get a Perfect Preacher
How to Build a Foolproof Bomb Shelter

Pray for them instead of bad-mouthing them, God seemed to say.

"But Lord, how do I pray for a mess like that?" I asked.

Just let Me pray it through you, came the simply reply. Then it came like this:

"Lord Jesus, You have officiated at the Baptismal ceremony of Methodists, Episcopalians, Lutherans, and in fact, just about all sizes and shapes of religious folks. Why can't You do it to just one Baptist preacher in the City of Baltimore? Just equip one of them with all the gifts of Your Holy Spirit in evidence in his ministry, Lord. They just can't be all that hard for You to handle."

Our little group of charismaniacs prayed that prayer seven nights a week for four years, and then the miracle happened. Pastor Frank Downing of Belvedere Baptist Church began acting in a most peculiar manner, conducting a healing service every Thursday morning right in the church, and people were getting healed all over the place.

We got just what we asked for—a pastor with all nine gifts of the Holy Spirit in evidence in his ministry. You should ask Brother Frank to tell you about it sometime.

Of course, I wanted to leave my old dead Baptist church right away and join the like-minded brethren of Belvedere Baptist. But the Lord said, *Hill, I'm not through with you in your present fellowship. In fact, you won't be ready to leave until you're willing to stay.*

Three years later, I had accepted the church where I was and had finally learned the really great lesson of respecting other folks' right to be wrong. Then I was free to leave, rejoicing, and join the Belvedere Baptist Church where today over 90 percent of the membership have met Jesus as Baptizer as well as Savior, with the New Testament evidence of speaking with new tongues.

Isn't Jesus wonderful?

More and more I'm more than willing to trust God with everything, because I've seen what He can do. There was a time, not so long ago, when a lot of people in our area were building bomb shelters. Baltimore is a prime target area because of our industry and the proximity of Washington.

And so one day, my business partner said, "I think I've done something that will make you unhappy. I've called in a contractor to build us an underground bomb shelter at the plant."

"Well," I said, "that doesn't make me unhappy at all."

"It doesn't?"

"Well, no. If you feel that you need a bomb shelter underground, by all means, build one. But don't bother to put any room in it for me. I don't want a cell underground. I don't need that, because I have a promise from God." I had come across this Scripture: "For thou hast been . . . a refuge from the storm, a shadow from the heat, when the blast of the terrible ones is as a storm against the wall" (Isa. 25:4).

My God says, "Depend on Jesus." The stormy blast doesn't frighten me.

How to Fly Through a Fog
How to Get a Perfect Preacher
How to Build a Foolproof Bomb Shelter

I looked over the plans and saw that the specifications for the bomb shelter included a shotgun—to shoot the neighbors when they tried to break in and find shelter in our bomb shelter. We didn't have room to share with them, so we had to be prepared to shoot them if they became too belligerent about joining us.

"Go ahead and build your bomb shelter," I told my partner, "and equip it with your shotgun, and feel free after a couple of weeks, or months, when the blast has cooled a little bit, to come out and eat burnt grass, and burnt dogs and cats, and burnt neighbors' kids. But count me out. I don't need it. Jesus is my shelter from the stormy blast. Hallelujah!"

Do you think I want to stay underground for a week, or a month, and come out in a rat race? I'm going straight up. Isn't that better?

Of course, there are anxious moments, but they don't last when you begin to praise Jesus for His immediate presence and His immediate power. I don't mean somewhere far off, in the distant future. I mean right now. Right here. If the kingdom is in us, as He says it is, then the things of the Kingdom—righteousness, peace, and joy —will spill out of us, right here, right now, in our own experience as we live the victory.

22
How to Get Your Whole Family
Saved and Healed

One day I started out for a retreat in Wheeling, West Virginia, and as I drove along, I said, "Lord, it would sure be nice to have a fresh word of testimony for the meeting tonight." That's where I made my first mistake. As many times as I've learned it, it didn't enter my head just then that in order to get a fresh word of testimony, you've got to be freshly delivered from something, and in order to be freshly delivered from something, you've first got to get in trouble. So I was headed for trouble. I'd asked for it.

It was a beautiful day, and I was rolling down the Pennsylvania Turnpike about seventy miles an hour, praising the Lord. I was confident that my car, tires and all, was in super-perfect condition. I had just had new tires put on, oversized snow tires, to be prepared for any weather.

Suddenly, without any warning at all, one of my tires blew out. I heard it pop, and I felt it. Man, how I felt it!—a sudden drop of a half foot on one of the rear wheels, and the car was completely out of control, sliding sideways down the Pennsylvania Turnpike on Friday afternoon with heavy truck traffic and cars everywhere I looked—so many I couldn't count them.

Then all at once, unexplainably, the traffic was out of my way. It was as if a giant hand moved everything ahead of me because I needed the whole highway to myself. I was all over it, with the tires whistling and shrieking, just like you always hear before the big crash.

What did I do? Panic? Put my hands over my ears and brace myself for the crunch? Oh, no.

"Hallelujah, Lord! It's graduation day! I'm coming right up to see You."

As I praised Him, I was reminded that graduation day was fine, but I didn't have to graduate on Slue Foot's terms. There'd be no glory for God in that. And so I prayed, "Lord, if I graduate today, there's no way I can go on down to Wheeling to tell them how wonderful You are. If I'm to be in a casket at the undertaker's, You've lost me as a witness for this event tonight. Which way do You want it, Lord? It's all the same to me. Doesn't make a particle of difference—"

Jesus said that what we loose on earth is loosed in heaven, and I loosed the whole situation to Him. I didn't bind it up by any anxiety, and He was free to manipulate by His supernatural power and deliver me. In the split seconds while I was still whistling sideways at seventy miles an hour, the word of the Lord came to my rescue:

In the name of Jesus is all power in heaven and earth. Use My name. I've given you the power of attorney to use My name in every situation.

At once, I began to speak His name out loud: "Jesus. Jesus." And I could feel the powers of darkness depart from the situation. Old Slue Foot had to take off in a hurry, because he cannot stand the name of Jesus.

The car straightened up and began to whip from side to side. I knew the big snow tire was just wrapping itself around the wheel and unwrapping. My steering wheel didn't do me a bit of good, because the power steering was all out of control, with the wheels not being on the ground solidly enough to do any good. But I kept praising Jesus, telling Him it was His problem. And He brought that car to a perfectly safe stop right at the Somerset exit.

In a few minutes, I had a new tire on and was back on the highway, praising the Lord—for the fresh word of testimony with which He had blessed me. I wouldn't have chosen that method to get it. But there it was. God had delivered.

Not every deliverance from trouble is accomplished as quickly as changing a flat tire on an interstate highway, however. Somewhere along the line we have to learn patience to trust God when everything looks like it is out of *His* control as well as ours. I learned it the hard way—in the midst of a nightmare family situation.

I have a wife and a daughter and a granddaughter, and

I was very proud of *my* wife Ruth, *my* daughter Linda, and *my* granddaughter Lisa, better known as Sweet-Pea. Then one day we almost lost our daughter because she was our very own possession. Now I'm delighted that she is Jesus' property and not mine. He can take care of His own. I'll tell you how it came about.

One day, after years of interfering and trying to get my family saved by my own efforts, I came across Acts 16:31: "Believe on the Lord Jesus Christ, and thou shalt be saved, *and thy house.*" I had never seen those last three words before. I had skipped right over them. I had my household completely churned up, disturbed. I was preaching at them, Bible slapping, and being a general nuisance, doing the best I could with my own efforts, totally ignoring God's means of bringing people into the kingdom. But that day the words leaped out at me: "and thy house."

I said, "Lord, when did You add that to my Bible? That means the household of a saved man is guaranteed membership in the Royal Family!"

And it seemed as if the Lord said, *Of course. Your part is to claim it every morning. But don't just do it one time, if you want it to happen in a hurry.*

And so, every morning I'd open up to Acts 16:31, put my finger on it, hold it up so God could see it good and clear, and say, "Lord, You said it. How about doing it?"

And I'd close the book and go on about my business. I never said another witnessing word to my wife or my daughter, and in a few weeks, my wife was saved. And my wife was the hardest kind to get saved—a fifty-year-old Episcopal woman, who had once represented all the spirituality we had in our family.

After my wife was saved, one Sunday morning our daughter almost shocked both of us to death. She got up and said, "Mother, I think I'll go with you to church this morning." She had never voluntarily done such a thing in her nineteen years. We tried not to show our enthusiasm, because you can blow it that way, you know.

That very day, a rare event took place in the church. A guest speaker, freshly back from the mission field and on fire for Jesus, had been invited to fill the pulpit. That young missionary preached salvation, loud and clear.

My teenage daughter heard him out and stayed after the service to talk to him. After a brief counseling session with the missionary, she began to show interest in things spiritual and started attending our prayer group meetings with us. She soon gave her heart to Jesus in one of those meetings. Later, Tommy Tyson came to Baltimore and clinched it, bringing her into total dedication.

Linda was an active fencer, and at a tournament she met a champion fencer who was a student at the Naval Academy in Annapolis, Maryland. After his graduation, they were married. He was on the Olympic Team, and naturally she left Baltimore to travel with him. It was big-time stuff for a budding admiral and his bride.

In the midst of all the excitement, our daughter got all

the way away from God, and seemed to have forgotten Him completely. But when His finger is on you, when the Hound of Heaven is on your trail, you'll never get away. Might as well give up. Praise the Lord.

But we didn't know that truth, then. We were concerned, and we were anxious for our daughter. By our anxiety, we were binding her. We had not learned to loose her, and so we became a big part of the problems that began to mount in her life.

We tried to straighten things out for them, tried to live their lives. But our solutions to their problems fell flat, and soon the young people were on the verge of divorce.

My daughter, in true Hill fashion, chose a jar of a thousand deadly poison tablets of aspirin as the solution to her problems and began to chew on them. When discovered, she had enough of that stuff in her system to kill the whole neighborhood. She was taken to the Naval Academy Hospital, and they looked at her and said, "She won't live till morning. We don't have the facilities even to try to help her."

After an hour's ambulance ride, she was admitted to Bethesda Naval Hospital. There, the doctors told us, "We've done all we can. She cannot live until morning."

Well, now, it's one thing to talk about prayer in a prayer group, and it's another thing to try to pray when your daughter is dying. That gets real personal. And the typical prayer of unbelief, "Lord, heal her if it be Thy will," is not good enough. Just then, I'm not after God's will. I'm after *my* will. Because when your young'un is dying, you're not thinking about God's will. You don't care what God wants. You want your kid to live, and so did we.

Mama and I didn't try to fool ourselves or God. We said, "Lord, we've got to play it our way. We can't help it. It's got to be a selfish prayer. Lord, heal our daughter. Deliver our daughter, Lord. She's our only child."

That's the best we could do. We prayed amiss, and nothing happened. We prayed with our understanding, but we didn't understand anything. We had forgotten for a minute what God says in Romans 8:26, that we don't know how to pray or what to pray for. We overlooked praying in the Spirit, letting the Holy Spirit intercede for us. But finally, we tried that, and began to pray in tongues, and stopped wrecking the situation by injecting our own biased opinion, our own will.

And the Spirit interceded for our daughter, according to the will of God, with groanings that cannot be uttered. And as we prayed in the Spirit, the Lord seemed to speak within us, asking the question, *Whose child are you praying for?*

"Ours, Lord."

Then it seemed as if the Lord said, *If you're praying for your child, prepare for a funeral. But if you're praying for My child, prepare for a miracle. What you bind on earth by 'my this' and 'my that' is bound in heaven, and I can't do a thing for you. But what you loose on earth, what you lay on the altar and turn over to Me—in that, I work a miracle because I'm a miracle-working God. All you have to*

*do is give your daughter to Me and acknowledge that
you're powerless to do anything.*

Medically, she was hopeless. Not a chance to live twenty-
four hours.

We knew we were powerless, and we confessed it.
"Lord, we can't do anything." And we released our daugh-
ter to Him. "Lord, we're glad that she's Your young'un.
You loaned her to us for a few years, and we messed her
up real good. If we hadn't, she wouldn't be in this mess.
How are You going to get Your young'un out of this mess?
Hallelujah!"

At that instant, a miracle took place. The medical record at Bethesda Naval Hospital contains the chart of the
inevitable, irreversible deterioration—that suddenly flat-
tened off. The acid level stopped rising, and never went
up one more point. It went away, though things like that
don't go away.

After her recovery, Linda told us, "At the crisis point,
when several doctors were working over me, I became
aware that I had a clear choice between life and death. I
sensed a great concern for me in all the people who were
working so hard to save the life I no longer wanted. And
in the middle of the dark tunnel in which I seemed to be
walking, I chose to return to life—even though I had been
determined to die."

Today Linda praises God that we were willing to release her. She knows that was what enabled Jesus to
move instantly and miraculously, even though it was already medically "too late."

The doctors were so certain they'd misread the meters or something, they kept her for seven more weeks in the psychiatric ward, just watching. They called it "something that cannot be explained in medical terms, an unexplained reaction to a deadly poison." Won't that pass for a miracle? It couldn't happen until we loosed her.

We lost our daughter that night, but we gained a sister. I lost my wife that night. I gained a sister. She lost a husband that night. She gained a brother. You can't believe the difference in relationship in our home when we learned to loose one another on the altar before Jesus and say, "Lord, You minister to this young'un of Yours." I thought she was my possession, and it almost killed her. I was so glad to find out she was the King's kid, and the King can certainly take care of His own property. I've learned to let Him do it. Ownership demands our all— Stewardship sets us free. Hallelujah!

23
How to Fix Expensive Machinery—Fast

Soon after Jesus baptized me in the Spirit, I had an opportunity to see how the supernatural works in the scientific world. I was called in on a case in Baltimore involving a power station. We had furnished the heavy power equipment, and part of our contract had to do with checking it out prior to turning it over to the city.

One morning I received an urgent phone call: "We are in difficulty, because at one o'clock this afternoon, this power station has to be turned over to the mayor and the city council—and it will not function."

"Well," I said, "this is a fine time to call me—about four hours before it has to operate perfectly."

They were apologetic. "We thought we could find the trouble. We've had the technicians from General Electric and our own technicians working for two weeks, but we're stumped. What are you going to do about it?"

Well, praise the Lord, I had a consultant, the best in the

business, Jesus Himself. I had been led to believe that He could provide, by the supernatural gifts of the Spirit, a word of knowledge, a word of wisdom, and discernment—the first three gifts of I Corinthians 12. A word of wisdom is knowing what to do next. A word of knowledge is knowing how to do it. And the discerning of spirits, or the discerning of the situation, is a clear readout. I would trust the Holy Spirit to give me the gifts I needed. So I said to the man on the phone. "I'll be right up and find the trouble."

"No," he said, "don't move. You stay right there, and I'll be down and pick you up." He was afraid for me to leave the office. He didn't want me to disappear, because many hundreds of thousands of dollars depended on that thing working within four hours.

I began to pray, and immediately, while I was praying, I knew exactly what was wrong. I saw it as clearly as a picture on a TV screen. This was my first experience with diagnosing a serious and complicated electronic problem strictly by the Holy Spirit, and Satan said, "You crazy fool. You're just imagining that. It's too ridiculous." But I was too dumb to doubt the Word of God.

I walked into the power station, directed entirely by the Holy Spirit. I had used the programming gifts—tongues, interpretation of tongues, and prophecy—to enable me to receive a program from God to know what to do. And so I walked over to the spot that I had seen in the Spirit as being the trouble source and issued instructions to the technicians as to what to do to cure it.

They said, "Mr. Hill, we've been through all that. We've checked it all out."

I said, "You called me in here as a consultant. Are you going to carry out my instructions? If not, I'm going back to the office."

One of them said, "Yes, sir." Although what I suggested seemed absurd, they had nothing else to try. So they did what I told them, pushed the button, threw the switches, and the thing took off like it was supposed to—to my amazement as well as theirs. I breathed a sigh of relief, and my knees shook a little bit to think what might have happened had nothing happened. I didn't realize until afterward how ridiculous it must have seemed, for me to walk in with about twenty highly trained engineers and technicians who had been baffled for weeks, and put my finger on the trouble immediately. Normally, this would bring a question from somebody. It had to. And it did.

As I was walking out, one of the General Electric technicians said, "Pardon me, sir, but could I ask you a question?"

I said, "Of course. I'll be glad to try to answer it."

"How could you possibly walk in here—you've never been here before, because we've been on the job night and day—how could you walk in and find this trouble when we were baffled by it?"

Satan said, "If you say you prayed about it, they'll think you're out of your mind." So I just looked wise and walked out, taking full credit for the wisdom God gave me.

I blew it—a fantastic opportunity to witness to Jesus' present-day power— and for four or five days I was really tormented. Satan kept accusing me: "You see? You're not ever going to make a witness. You might as well give up. Why, you blew your assignment completely. God will give up on you now, sure as anything. He'll never trust you with anything else." And I believed what Satan said and was full of remorse and torment.

But then one day I just happened to read Romans 8:1: "There is therefore now no condemnation to them which are in Christ Jesus." And I asked myself, "Where does that condemnation come from if it's not the Lord?" And I got the message. Slue Foot, the father of lies. It wasn't God who was condemning. He makes allowances for my goofs. And I said, "Lord, I thank You. I really praise You that You're a forgiving God, not a condemning God."

And I said, "Lord, give me another opportunity, and by Your grace, I won't blow it."

The next opportunity came in an unusual way. We do a lot of maintenance work in connection with the army communication systems, microwave installations, short-wave things, and they're all quite intricate. There came a call one day for an emergency inspection and correction trip to one of their installations down in Virginia. We made an appointment for our chief electronics man to go, but the day before he was supposed to go, he had an accident that put him out of commission. So I had to call the office at the Corps of Engineers in Virginia to wipe out that appointment and arrange another one. As I was waiting for the call to go through, it seemed as if the Lord said, *Why don't you go down, Hill?*

I said, "Lord, I'm ah-ra-ah-ra—" I tried to weasel out of it.

He said, *You've been bragging about how I could find and correct any trouble, haven't you?*

I said, "That's right."

Well, why don't you go down there and find out if I really can?

Now that's coming close to home, isn't it? But then I began to get excited over the prospect. So when the call went through, I said, "I'm calling to request a change of personnel on the passes that you've issued for the trip tomorrow. Change the name from so and so to my name, because our other technician is unable to be there."

And he said, "Who are you?"

"Well, I'm president." That'll get you in anywhere, whether you know anything or not.

He said, "Oh, very well." He didn't sound too enthusiastic, because most presidents may not know a whole lot about the technical details, and I'm one of them. I know very little about the intricacies of microwave. But I would go representing the Chief Technician of the universe, the One who is all wisdom and knowledge. It would be exciting to see how Jesus was going to bail me out of this one.

I arrived at Alexandria, Virginia, at the Corps of Engineers station, and they gave me three technicians. They said, "This will probably be a long, involved process. We'll check you out for return at eight o'clock this evening." They figured on a full day's trip, travel, plus time on the job to locate and correct the trouble.

That was reasonable, by human standards. But they didn't know that I was tuned in to the Head Man of the universe. And on the way down to that station, as I was praying in tongues, I had seen in the spirit what was wrong with the equipment. That beats trying to diagnose a malfunction by normal processes.

God always has information at His fingertips that you can never get by ordinary means. He always knows one more fact about things than you'll ever know. I had prayed in tongues. The interpretation came by word of knowledge and a clear picture—discernment of the trouble.

The technicians said, "Since we're apt to be here for several hours, why don't we have lunch first and then go in and check the thing out?"

"Well," I said, "if it's all the same to you, let's get it on the air right now and head back for Alexandria. Wouldn't you like to get back early?"

They said, "Yes, but how are you going to do that? You're going to have to find the trouble first."

"Oh," I said, "I know the trouble already. It'll take about five minutes to fix it."

"Five minutes! Mister Hill, do you realize we've had the experts from Pentagon over here? We've had the manufacturer's people down here? We've had this thing checked from end to end, and every time we push the button, it blows fourteen hundred dollars worth of high-powered microwave transmitter tubes?"

They were nervous wrecks because they had to check out those new tubes on their cost tickets. And the price of that station was higher than any other one in the whole world—a bushel of tubes every time they fired up. No wonder they were nervous.

There was no way I could reassure them. I said again, "Five minutes will do it."

They were looking at me as if they were wondering about my sanity. "You sure you know what you're doing?"

I said, "Did you get me down here to play games?"

"No, sir."

"If you'll do what I tell you, we'll be out of here in less than fifteen minutes, all tested out."

Well, it sounded too good to be true, and they decided to find out what kind of a screwball I was. So they went along with the gag. That was their attitude. They looked at each other and one of them said, "All right. What do we do?"

"Take those cover plates off the main alternator."

"Mister Hill, we have checked that whole thing. It's all been—"

I said, "Take the coverplates off. Do you want to play games, or do you want results?"

They took the coverplates off.

I said, "Now loosen that set screw. Turn that brush rig back one inch to the left."

"But Mister Hill, it's on the factory markings. We will be penalized for touching that because the factory has—"

I said, "Turn it back one inch, or I'll do it. Do you want me to do it?"

Their Adam's apples were bobbing up and down as they tried to swallow their apprehensions. "No, sir. No, sir," they chorused. "We're the technicians."

"Well, then, turn it back."

"Yes, sir."

"Tighten it up."

"Yes, sir."

"Put the covers back on."

"Yes, sir."

"Now push the button."

"No, sir!! We're not pushing any buttons. That thing will blow up in our face!"

I said, "Stand outside the door then." And they did. They were glad to. I pushed the button. Things fired up. The station went on the air. I said, "Let's go back to Alexandria." And they just stood there sweeping their eyeballs up.

We got in the car, and they gulped, and one of them nudged the other, and I knew that they were trying to work up courage to ask me how I did it. I was waiting for the questions.

Finally one of them said, "Would you mind if we asked you a question?"

"No. Indeed, no. If I can answer it." I knew what was coming.

"Would you tell us, would you please tell us how you could come down here, put your finger right on the trouble, and correct it, when we've been sweating this thing for weeks? We've had orders from the top brass to get that thing on the air and keep it on the air, and we just couldn't do it. It was beyond us. How did you do it?"

I settled back in my seat. "I'm glad you asked the question, gentlemen, because on the way down here I prayed about it and God showed me exactly what to do." All the way back to Alexandria, a two-hour trip or so, I told them about Jesus. They had asked a question, they were entitled to an answer.

I gave the answer as the Spirit led me. And I didn't have to worry or wonder about how they would receive it. That was the Holy Spirit's business, not mine.

Something King's kids have to learn about witnessing, about praying for healing or anything else, is that the power is God's, not our own. He's the one responsible for the harvest. We're not to judge for ourselves even the wisdom or unwisdom of what we say when we're moving in the Spirit, because His ways are not our ways, and His thoughts are far above our thoughts. Our reliance has to be on His Word, never on our feelings about it. And where we leave it all up to Him, He'll get the victory every time.

24
How to Win Arguments with Intellectuals

We all know that God knows much more than we can ever
dream of knowing. But most of the time we're a little slow
in giving Him an opportunity to get His knowledge through
to us that His name might be glorified. But whenever I've
asked Him for wisdom—that His name might be glorified—He's *never* failed to give it.

I had an invitation not long ago to talk to a group of scientists in Trenton, New Jersey. These men all held PhD degrees in their own professions, top scientists, mostly working in physics or chemistry in various universities and research laboratories. Every month they would invite a speaker to come talk on almost any subject. Like the people Paul
found on Mars Hill, they were interested in hearing about
any new thing. Philosophy was an all-right subject with
them, and so was religion. Except for two or three of the
men, most of them were devout pagans.

There were fifteen or so scientists, eggheads, gathered in

a living room that night. As I began to share some of my experiences with them, two of them appeared to be especially interested in what I had to say. I didn't know why until I had talked for about ten minutes, and then one of them challenged me.

"You Christians talk a good game, I'll admit, but that's as far as it goes," he said. "You don't *do* anything about what you believe. I'm a pacifist, and as far as I can see, you Christians are all a bunch of phonies. If you have the power to change circumstances that you claim to have, why don't you get out and do something about ending wars, for instance?"

And then his friend across the room—it turned out they were in league together—chimed in. "Yeah, if you so-called Christians lived it instead of just talking it to death, we wouldn't have all these problems—wars and all that kind of thing."

They kept the conversation going back and forth between themselves, and I could see the whole evening was ruined as far as the Lord was concerned, because I was no match for them. They were intellectual giants compared to me. The second man was a professor of philosophy. Obviously, it would have been a waste of time for me to try to straighten him out, because I'd have been straightened out in about two minutes.

As they passed the atheistic and pacifistic ball back and forth between themselves, I began to pray. "Lord, this meeting is finished unless You intercede." I could tell that my other Christian friends were on the hot line to heaven just as I was, praying in tongues.

On a commonsense level, we'd have packed up and gone home. Finished. But King's kids know nothing about defeat. All they understand is victory. We know we're always confronting an already defeated adversary, and we're specialists in dealing with him. Satan cannot intercept our praying in tongues. It's all Greek to him.

So, a perfectly untampered-with prayer, a Holy Spirit prayer, sped to the throne of grace, and God responded with a word of knowledge, a readout that came through as clear as a photograph. Suddenly I saw something about the pacifist who was speaking so forcefully, so sure of himself, so in command of the situation. I saw something about him that nobody else in that room knew except himself. God had tuned me in on the information supernaturally, given me a word of knowledge. It gave me the upper hand, but God seemed to say, *Just wait. First let him state his position. Then you step in.*

It became very exciting as I sat there and tried to keep from bursting out laughing, waiting for the right moment. So I let the pacifist run on as long as he was fluent, and when he stopped for breath, I said, "Pardon me, sir. Could I ask you a question?" He was very magnanimous, ready to grant me any wish that my heart might desire. He and his friend were confident they had built a beautiful case against Christians, me in particular.

I said, "You claim to be a pacifist in every sense of the word, is that right?"

"Oh yes, indeed. Oh yes, indeed."

"There's no doubt about it? There's no area of your life in which you are not a pacifist, is that true?"

"That's entirely true."

"Sir, would you happen to have a loaded gun in your home?"

I saw it, you see, in the Spirit. God had let me look into the pacifist's hall closet, and He showed me a loaded rifle there.

The man turned as white as a sheet and began to sputter. "That's beside the point."

"Oh no, sir. That's not beside the point—that's right exactly on the point. We are talking about pacifism. Pacifism means no guns. None." I repeated my question.

"Sir, do you have a loaded gun—a rifle—in your home—in your hall closet?"

He had to answer. And he did, but not loud.

"Yes."

Wow! I could feel the power of Satan shrivel.

"Sir, you are not a pacifist. You're a three-dollar bill—as phony as they come. A double-talker, entirely out of order, mouthing pacifism with a loaded gun in your home."

The man slumped down in the corner of his chair. There was not one more word out of him all evening. I talked about Jesus, and they listened, impressed by this obvious invasion of the meeting by God Himself.

But that's not the end of the story.

The next day, the pacifist-scoffer telephoned the couple at Princeton who had accompanied me to the meeting. He said, "God was in that meeting last night."

"That's a strange statement for someone who doesn't believe in the supernatural gifts of God," was the reply.

"Well," he said, "I *didn't,* but I'm sure now that God was there, because I am a master at holding onto a conversation. Nobody can take it away from me, especially that stupid engineer Hill."

"That's absolutely right. Wouldn't you like to know that kind of God more intimately?" came the question.

Not long thereafter, that philosophy professor met Jesus as his personal Baptizer in the Holy Spirit.

He had previously met Jesus as his personal Savior, but his EIB had prevented his experiencing the power of Jesus in his life to meet the needs of others.

This scoffer became one of the sweetest brothers in the Lord I have ever met, and the next time I saw him, he hugged my neck and said, "Thank You, Jesus."

Doing battle on the level of the intellect would have been unfruitful. No one would have been saved or changed. Someone might have said, "What a wonderful message!" and I'd have known that I'd really goofed it, making myself the center of attraction.

But when, after I have spoken, someone says, "What a wonderful Savior!" I know that Jesus has been lifted up to draw all men unto Himself.

For it is not by might and mind-power, not by three points and a poem, but "by My Spirit," saith the Lord, that He convinces unbelievers, and turns them into King's kids.

25
How to Heal by Proxy

One of the things I've learned to be thankful for is my own
ignorance in the problem areas that are brought to me for
ministry. If I thought I knew something about a problem, I
might prescribe a wrong cure. But when in my weakness, in
my utter ignorance, I'm forced to rely on God's knowledge,
His strength is made perfect in my weakness. He proves
that the foolishness of God is far better than the wisdom of
men.

Several years ago, a group of doctors, nurses, and medical
technicians in Baltimore, the Christian Medical Fellowship,
asked me to come and talk to their group. They had heard
I'd had some experience with healing. I suppose there were
fifteen or twenty people there, coming and going, because
some of them were on duty or on call. But there was one doctor I noticed who was there the whole evening, without in-
terruption.

I told some of my experiences in healing, how I had been

healed, and had seen healing happen to others. Toward the end of the evening, the one who had been so attentive throughout said, "I have a patient who is critically ill. Do you suppose that God could heal her at a distance?"

We checked the Manufacturer's Handbook and found that Jesus had healed the centurion's servant from a distance, without ever even seeing him. And Jesus had said that we would do the same things He had done, and even greater things because He had gone to the Father, and so we took that as our authority to believe that Jesus still heals at a distance today. He says, "I'm the same yesterday, today, and forever. I change not."

Well, Satan was present in the meeting to try to discourage us, to instill fear of failure. "You're going to blow this one, now," he whispered. "You're in a group of medical people. What right have you to come here and talk about healing? These people are all professionals." I could feel him sneering at me.

I told him, as I always do, "Everything you say is true." I agreed quickly with my adversary. "I am not qualified to come and talk to medical people, but Jesus is the great Physician, and He is in me. Now go away, Satan. Don't bother me. I'm busy on my Father's business."

"Yes, of course Jesus still heals at a distance," I assured the doctor.

"Then I would like to sit in the prayer chair as a proxy for a patient of mine who is critically ill." That's all he told us, and that's all we needed to know.

He had not revealed his standing, whether he himself was a Christian or not. He had simply expressed his concern for a critically ill patient, and that was enough. Jesus healed unbelievers. He healed many people who didn't even know that He was healing them.

The doctor sat in the chair, and we took the Manufacturer's Handbook and began at Romans 8:14, putting ourselves in a position to be led by the Spirit of God. We acknowledged that we didn't know how to pray or what to pray for. It was entirely up to Him. "Lord, You take it from here."

We began to pray in tongues, and as I laid hands on the doctor, I got a readout in the form of a complete picture of a nervous system in a person—like an X ray, except that X rays do not reveal nerves. This picture did. It showed the nervous system completely out of balance. On one side of the body it was like an overtuned violin, with all the strings under tremendous tension, pulling, twisting, distorting. On the other side, all the strings were dangling, unwound, not tuned at all.

I heard myself praying, "Lord, please heal this person of nervous imbalance." As soon as the words came out of my mouth, I was embarrassed. What a kooky sounding thing that was—nervous imbalance. I'd never heard of such a thing.

Satan got my ear in a hurry. "Hill, you really goofed that one. Nervous imbalance! There's no such thing." His guffaws of derision were loud in my ear, and I'll never forget the look of total disgust on the doctor's face. I could tell that he was completely turned off by the whole thing.

But King's kids are not supposed to be impressed by negatives, because our God is a miracle-working God. And He doesn't goof. So the Spirit of praise came to my assistance. God promises us the garment of praise for the spirit of heaviness. And so I said, "Lord, I praise You. I thank You. If I've goofed it, You're still the redeeming God. If I've misread the signs and prayed the wrong thing, that's Your problem. You got me into this business. You're going to have to redeem it. Hallelujah!" And I was set free from condemning myself.

Shortly thereafter, I received a request to attend another session. I just happened to be free, so I went back. That night there was a young PhD philosophy graduate there, and he was quite interested in all I had to say. But he didn't agree with me.

"I can just as easily prove that God is dead as you Christians can prove He's alive," he said.

With that, the doctor who had sat in proxy for prayer for his critically ill patient spoke up. "Young man, I happen to have a report for the group here tonight that proves that God is alive. Last week I sat in the prayer chair for a patient of mine who was critically ill. Three of us doctors had consulted about her just the day before. We had told her that we had done all we could do. Medically, we could do no more except remove most of her insides and install artificial plumbing. She might just as well forget that she was a young woman, because the operation was going to ruin her body. It was the best we could offer, because she had a spastic bladder. That's incurable medically."

Then the doctor turned to me and continued. "When you prayed for the healing of a nervous imbalance, I thought that was as weird as anything could be, because every doctor knows that spastic organs have nothing to do with nervous imbalance. But when I examined that patient the next morning, I found every symptom of that spastic organ gone. They've stayed gone for a week. She is completely healed. In the meantime, I have begun to check out the connection between spastic organs and nervous imbalance, and I find we had totally overlooked a whole area of medical research. I'm starting on it right away."

Relying on God's knowledge instead of our own intelligence—or lack of it—is a sure road to blessing. It's part of living like a King's kid.

26
How to Become Demon-Possessed
How to Deliver from Demons

A frequent topic of discussion in the midst of the charismatic renewal is demon possession. Maybe you don't think these things happen today. I don't have any theories about the subject, but I've had some experiences that coincide with what I've read in the Bible. When a King's kid sees God's word confirmed in the world, nobody's theology is going to persuade him that his eyes are making things up.

Many years ago, before I became a Christian, my wife became demon-possessed. She had been a spiritist medium for years. I was in college when I first met her, and she was deeply involved in doing automatic writing. She could hold a pencil on a piece of paper, and it would start writing words. We thought it was cute. She had been dabbling in the occult for a long time, had graduated from Ouija boards by the time she was ten.

We were married a couple of years after I graduated. I was

179

a young engineer starting out in the world of industry. I had a head full of education, and I soon learned how little I knew.

I would come home baffled at night. My job was too big for me. I had suddenly become chief engineer when my boss had been transferred. I lacked the knowledge and the experience necessary to solve the engineering problems. And so I was on the verge of being a wreck.

One night my wife said, "Why don't we consult some of my 'friends' and get some answers?"

At first I didn't know what she was talking about.

"What do you mean?" I asked.

She said, "We'll sit down in the living room after dinner, and we'll have a session with my 'friends,' you know, the spirits." She didn't even have to go into a trance, she was so highly developed. She saw the spirits and communicated verbally with them. "Here they come," she said.

I said, "Where?"

She said, "Don't you see them?"

"I certainly don't."

"Don't you hear them?"

"No, I don't."

But she did, and she said, "State your question." I stated the question, my engineering problem, in technical engineering terms.

And my wife said, "I don't know what you're talking about." Then she turned to her friends and said, "Do you know what he means?" And then she'd tell me, "Yes, they say they know what you mean." We waited for a few minutes, and they came back with an answer, and I went to the office the next day and tried it out—and it worked! So it became a regular habit with me to take my engineering problems home with me and have my wife ask her 'friends' for the solution to them. I never saw the 'friends,' never was able to hear them, because I had a Christian mother who put me under the blood of Jesus. That made the difference. My wife had, by her occult involvement, left herself wide open for the exercise of Satanic power.

After our daughter was born, my wife began to act in a very peculiar manner. Soon she turned suicidal. One day her psychiatrist told me, "The day will come when she will threaten to destroy a member or two of your family—it could be you. When that happens, call me immediately. I will have made preparations."

The day came, and for a year, I didn't have a wife. I had an insane person locked up in an insane asylum. She wasn't really insane, she was demon-possessed, but we didn't know about such things then. The psychiatrist didn't know. The doctors didn't know, because they were just Educated Idiots. Without Jesus, the most brilliant, the most highly trained man is nothing more than an Educated Idiot.

It was very dismal and grim having a new baby daughter and no mother for her. Her mother was locked up, possibly for life, because she had played with spooks. That's what Satan does to his people, he destroys them.

Time passed. Life was a painful blur. Then a doctor used

hypnosis on my wife and brought her out of her "insanity" into something more like normal. At the sanatorium, a doctor told me that possibly later in life, the sickness would return. I think that doctor knew about demons, but he didn't know how to tell me.

We were not Christians. Christians are under the protection of Jesus. The helmet of salvation protects their minds against voodoo and the invasion of evil spirits into their souls—unless they open their souls to Satanic invasion through willful dabbling in witchcraft or the occult. And many Christians do, being ignorant of the word of God.

"But I see nothing wrong with horoscopes, palm reading, Edgar Cayce, or seances," they say, because the EIB has no way of detecting demons until it's too late.

We saw nothing wrong with occult abominations, either, never having read the eighteenth chapter of Deuteronomy to understand it. I had done graduate work, even patented inventions. My Educated Idiot Box was in full control of my life, and though I could point to my wordly successes, I had an idiotic life and an empty stupid mind. I had never invited Jesus to move in. PhD, without Jesus, stands for posthole digger, going nowhere.

Without Jesus, and with her involvement with the occult, my wife stayed on the firing line of Satan. We didn't know it, of course, and ignorance of the enemy is exactly what he likes. In Christian Science, they taught me there is no Satan. That's his trick, to make you believe that he is not, that you're good, that there's no sin, and you don't need salvation. And I went to Unity, and Swedenborg, and metaphysics, and voodooism, and Yoga, and all the dismal, dreary religions and cults, but none of them could save my wife from insanity any more than they could pull me from the quick-mud I fell into when I was a boy.

One day, about seventeen years after her release from the mental hospital, I became aware that my wife was acting very peculiarly again. The violence hadn't set in as yet, but I knew it was on the way, because she was following the same pattern of strange behavior she had exhibited when our daughter was born in the thirties.

As I looked at her one day, suddenly I saw a face over the face of my wife, every bit as real as her own face, but it was the face of a horrible demon right out of the pits of hell. Not being trained in these things, I took her to a so-called Christian psychiatrist in Baltimore. But he'd never heard of the gifts of the Spirit—or of demons. When I told him what I had seen, he forgot my wife and went to work on me. I thought he was going to put me away.

The headshrinkers didn't have any answers. Where was there to go? Only one place. To the Lord.

Early in 1954, I met Jesus, and He baptized me, and equipped me with the gifts of the Holy Spirit. We dealt with that demon, bound it, and cast it out of my wife, and today she is perfectly normal. Praise God.

This time she'll stay that way, because we don't play with spooks at our house anymore.

Without the gifts of the Holy Spirit, my wife would be a

violent animal today. That's what the doctor said she would become, a violent animal. In other words, not a human being. If I had been a standard Southern Baptist, I would have had to settle for that, and that is Satanic. When our seminaries rob our young preachers of the knowledge of the activities of Satan plus the power gifts of the Holy Spirit to deal with those activities, it is a devilish thing. And our seminaries—our cemeteries, we should call them—are dealing out dead information.

In the Bible, I don't find anything about specialized deliverance ministries, but I do find normal Christians ministering deliverance, ministering healing, and ministering the gifts of the Spirit to bring wholeness and completeness to God's people. Without God's tool-kit, the gifts of the Holy Spirit, we are retarded Christians, falling back on that prayer of unbelief, "Lord, heal him if it be Thy will," and then calling the undertaker. King's kids *know* God's perfect will as stated in III John 2 is prosperity and health—there is no "if" about it.

One of the greatest moves of the Holy Spirit today among young people in Baltimore came about through the gifts of the Holy Spirit being exercised in our living room as my wife and I ministered to a psychologist.

I had witnessed to this man about ten years ago, and he didn't want any part of what I was talking about. He said, "That's all very fine for you, but I'm working on my master's, and I'll soon have my doctorate, and my psychology and psychiatric training is more than adequate for my needs."

So I had said, "I won't call you—you call me when you get ready to disintegrate."

How did I know he would? The insurance tables guarantee disintegration of the human mechanism in the early fifties. According to the insurance tables, if you're in the executive level of life, at age fifty-two and a half, you will have your first nervous breakdown or your first heart attack, or both. And I was following the pattern until I met Jesus.

About three years ago the psychologist called me one night, and he said, "I have a problem."

I said, "You have a what? I thought headshrinkers solved problems. I thought you had the answers, not the problems."

"Well," he said, "I thought so, too. But I have a problem."

"What is it?"

"Fear. Several years ago, you told me things that led me to believe that you have some influence with God. Could you help me?"

I said, "No, I couldn't help you, but Jesus could. If you're willing to be helped on His terms—or is your fear a hobby?"

"No, no, it's not a hobby. I'd like to get rid of it. It's kept me awake now for nearly a year."

Well, you see, I had him on my icky prayer list—that he'd never know any peace until he met the Prince of Peace.

He agreed that he was willing to do business on God's terms. He had no choice—except to get worse.

So he came over to the house, and my wife and I shared with him that we had found, in Jesus, deliverance from fear and anxiety. Deliverance from torment and guilt. Deliverance from emptiness of life, and the dreary drabness of existence without the living Savior.

Well, the pain and the misery on his face was a pretty clear indication of the torment inside. "Are you willing for Jesus to deliver you from your fear?"

He said, "I didn't know He could do that."

I said, "I didn't either, until it happened to me."

He said, "What do I have to do?"

I said, "Ask Jesus Christ to come into your heart, to be your Savior."

He did, and he was saved right there.

That made him eligible for the gifts God gives to King's kids.

So we laid hands on him and prayed in tongues. That's the telephone gift. "Lord, we don't know how to pray about this one. Please help us." I saw the spirit of fear locked up. Down in his insides, I saw a clear picture. And I knew that fear was of the devil.

We said, "Satan, in the name of Jesus Christ, we bind you, we cast you back to the pit where you came from. Take your hands off God's people and keep them off. In Jesus' name. Amen."

Fred sat up in the chair and felt himself all over. He said, "It's gone!"

"Well, that's what we were after, wasn't it? Didn't you want it to be gone?"

"Yes," he said, "but it went—"

"Well, of course it went—because King's kids are ministering to King's kids."

During the course of the evening, Fred felt himself every now and then to see if it would come back. But it didn't, because we had said, "Lord, seal him in Your Holy Spirit."

The next night Fred called and said, "It's still gone! It hasn't come back!"

"Well, isn't that what we put the order in for? Isn't that what we told Slue Foot? Go away and stay away. Of course. King's kids do that."

He said, "I want to know that kind of a God better. I want to be able to minister in that kind of power."

We invited him, and he came back over to the house. My wife and I laid hands on him, and Jesus baptized him in the Holy Spirit; he spoke in a new language and became a power-packed King's kid.

He had a wife and eleven children, and they all got saved. And they received the Baptism, and they got off of drugs and all the other chemical additives that you need without Jesus. Soon, they began to infiltrate into other kids' lives thereabouts. They started a little prayer group and a Bible study in their club basement, and the other kids began to come. Today, that group has grown into several hundred meeting at St. Joseph's parish house every Tuesday night—wall-to-wall young people, off of drugs and on to Jesus. Over the last several years, literally thousands have met Jesus Christ because Fred got delivered from fear.

This is the power of the Holy Spirit to empower ordinary Christians to get out there and act like God's people, in training for something greater beyond. I don't know how it could be greater, but He says it will be. The best is yet to come. Hallelujah!

27
How to Take Care of Crocodiles, Hippopotamuses, and Big Black Furry Things.

One of the most fantastic deliverances I have ever seen had to do with a dedicated, Spirit-filled Christian woman who became, as the psychiatrist said, totally and violently insane, tried to murder her best friend with a kitchen knife, and had to be put away in a mental institution. In the institution, she got steadily worse. Her body had swollen to twice its normal size, but the doctors could find nothing organically wrong with her. Finally, after several months, the doctors told her husband, "The best thing you can do is to forget you have a wife. She is hopelessly insane and will never recover."

Her husband was a senior at Princeton Theological Seminary, and this was during the time when the Holy Spirit was beginning to move at Princeton Seminary. There was a charismatic prayer group in the town. At first it met on the campus, later in a spacious home which was opened to them. Seminarians by the hundreds received the Baptism in the Holy Spirit there. Local residents also began to come, and the meeting became a home church second to none I've ever seen.

For a while, the husband attended the fellowship, but as the weeks went by, with a steady worsening of his wife's condition, he grew terribly discouraged and stayed away from the fellowship. He even decided to leave the ministry. He said, "I'm not sure I want to serve a God who steals wives." Then one night he happened to come back—a night when I was in the area—and stopped in for the prayer fellowship. He waited after the meeting until most of the folks had left—I guess there were ten or twelve of us remaining— and said, as sort of a final desperate cry for help, "I'd like to sit in the prayer chair for my wife, what's left of her." Of course, everybody had been praying already—hundreds of people, thousands of prayers. And his wife was still in the violent ward. There was no sign that any of the prayers were getting through.

But we didn't say, "Brother, thousands of prayers have already gone up. You've had your quota." We invited him to sit in the prayer chair, and we proceeded to follow the Manufacturer's Handbook, point by point. We said, "If the gifts of the Holy Spirit are worthless, just for interesting Sunday school talk, now is the time to find out." We knew we had a desperate situation. And we certainly didn't know how to pray or what to pray for. "Lord," we began, "the man's wife is insane. She's violent. She's sick. She needs help. The doctors say she's insane. Lord, what do You know about it?"

We were led to go directly to the Bible, the Manufacturer's Handbook at I Corinthians 12. We said, "Concerning spiritual gifts, Lord, we don't want to be ignorant."

Not be ignorant? We needed the first gift, a word of wisdom then, to know what to do, and we prayed in the Spirit, got on the hot line to heaven, prayed in tongues. And the word of wisdom came to us, saying, *Seek My word of knowledge, My people.*

"Lord, give us the word of knowledge. Give it to us in Your way." Then we prayed in tongues again. And the word of knowledge came, loud and clear. *The woman is not insane. Her actions are being controlled by demons.*

"Well, thank You, Lord. Now we're getting somewhere." The head doctors, the psychiatrists up there, the best specialists, had said she's insane. But they didn't know anything about demons. So the best they could do was goof it—at fifty dollars an hour. Insane? No, demon-controlled.

"All right, Lord, we thank You for the information. But how do we apply it?"

Well, He said, *you'll need the gift of faith for this one.*

That's the next gift—in verse nine, the gift of faith. "Thank You, Lord, for the gift of faith." We felt it rise right up within us. When the gift of faith rises up, you don't have to ask God, hopefully, to do something. It's unthinkable that He won't do what you're led to ask. The gift of faith overrides every fear, every uncertainty, and every anxiety. When

191

you're dealing with the powers of darkness, you need that gift.

"The gifts of healing are next," we said. "And the woman couldn't be sicker. God says that demons are causing her insanity—that's kind of a mess, isn't it? We need gifts of healing, all right.

"The next gift is the working of miracles, and if ever we needed the working of miracles, it's now, because the patient is about fifty miles away in the state hospital, and we're in the living room of a home." With God, there is no time or distance. Besides, the woman was in a locked ward. Nobody could go in to minister to her if they wanted to. But they didn't have to. King's kids have supernatural abilities beyond the natural.

"So Lord, we thank You for miracles, for Your glory."

Gifts of prophecy. The word of prophecy came, *I will heal. I am God. I deliver My people. Call on Me, and stand and see My salvation.* What's the word of prophecy for? To encourage and to correct. To comfort. We needed comfort, because we were getting into a shaky position. We'd never been here before. This was all brand-new. And the word of prophecy came right through and comforted us. God assured us, *You're on the right ground. Keep at it. Go ahead. Don't stop moving.* King's kids walk in and possess the land. Hallelujah!

Glory to Jesus! We began to get excited. And, naturally, Satan was right there to breathe in our ears. "You're wasting your time."

We said, "Go away, boy. We know better. We're on the

road, the victory road. Here we come, Satan. Get out of the way. Here come the King's kids."

"What's next, Lord?" Discerning of spirits—so that we can see the demons that we have to deal with, what Satan's doing, and what he's up to.

"Lord, please tell us how to discern the spirits."

And the word came back, *Call them by name.*

Well, that's a good idea. Jesus did that, didn't He? "In the name of Jesus Christ, Satan, reveal yourself."

Immediately I saw a clear picture, just like on TV—two pairs of eyes level with the surface of a swampy drainage ditch—dirty, swampy water. Grass growing out of it on either side like marsh grass. It was so vivid, I can see it still. The crocodile that had taken over her mind so that she tried to kill her friend with a kitchen knife, just as a crocodile rips and tears.

As we continued to say, "Satan, come out of there, reveal yourself," another pair of eyes came into view, eyes set far apart—eyes of a hippopotamus. A crocodile and a hippopotamus. No wonder her body had swollen to twice its normal size. No wonder she acted insane. Leviathan and behemoth, two demons controlling her. Both are mentioned in the Bible (see Job 40:15-24, 41:1-34). One of them took over the body, the other took over the mind. And the ailment of this woman was most unusual. Her body was swollen like a massive balloon and her mind, according to the doctors, was totally destroyed.

Knowing that Mark 16:17 was for us in such situations, we

were able to speak with authority, God's authority. We said, "Satan, in the name of Jesus Christ, come out of her."

And I saw the crocodile come up on the shore, turn over on his back with his yellow belly up in the air, and a drop of Jesus' blood hit him and he died, just like that.

The next morning, one of the members of the group who had not been at the prayer meeting and didn't know about our prayers went over to the hospital to check on the woman's condition. And the attendant at the desk said, "Well, you can visit her if you want to."

"Visit her! I thought she was—"

"Yes, but she was totally healed last night. There's nothing wrong with her mind, but her body is still blown up." And he walked into the room and the doctors and nurses were standing there, goggle-eyed.

Soon afterward, another member of the prayer fellowship visited her, laid hands on her, and said, "Be healed in the name of Jesus Christ," and that body swelling went down like a pricked balloon. When he told us, I recalled that we hadn't followed through with the hippopotamus that night. He had completed the job we had begun, and God brought total wholeness in two stages, much as Jesus did in healing the man born blind in Mark 8:23-25.

Discerning of spirits. Divers kinds of tongues. Interpretation of tongues. It took nine gifts to deliver the woman out of the mental hospital, to restore her to her husband.

Together, they wound up in the greatest ministry you ever heard of on the campus at the University of California among twenty-seven thousand pagans.

194

How to Take Care of Crocodiles,
Hippopotamuses, and Big Black
Furry Things

For seven years she's been as normal as anybody could be. And last summer I had the marvelous opportunity of seeing her and getting from her, her side of that experience, of how the demons had gotten in control. "The wrong use of the tongue," she confessed.

A little idle use of gossip. A little backbiting, a little resentment, talking about other folks. These demons ride up and down on your tongue instead of the spirit of praise and the spirit of thanksgiving. These ministering spirits are life or death, depending on where they come from, depending on their domain. And when you swallow with a mouthful of demons, you've got a stomach full of demons. And they get into your soul, although they can't take over the *spirit* of a Christian.

She said, "All the way through the experience, I knew I was saved, but I knew that my soul was filled with evil. And during that time, I was aware of the prayers of Christians. When a prayer group would pray in a concerted way, I would feel the relief, and when they'd stop praying, this suicidal and murderous demon would take over. And when the prayer in the group there that night came to cast out the demons, it was the first time I had been ministered to for deliverance by all the hundreds of Christians that had prayed."

We had not, because we had asked amiss. Without the tools of the Holy Spirit, the woman would still be violently insane or dead. And one of these days, possibly *Reader's Digest,* to which the manuscript was sent some time ago, will have the courage to publish an article about this case.

Soon after the seminarian's wife had been delivered and made whole, a man named Fred came to me and said, "I'm not sure about Satan. You know, that might have been just something that—" And he began to rationalize.

I said, "Lord, give him visible eyeball evidence of Satan's kingdom." It was the Holy Spirit praying that prayer, because I didn't half believe it myself when it came out of my mouth. But a few weeks later, Fred and I attended a retreat of Spirit-filled brethren in Baltimore.

One of them said, "I have been bothered by some kind of an unclean spirit. My mind is full of unclean thoughts, and I need deliverance."

We went into the prayer room, this brother, and Fred and I. We laid hands on this brother, and the power was so tremendous, I opened my eyes. As I did, I saw a big black furry thing come down his pants' leg out over his shoe top, run across the floor, and disappear down a crack. When the prayer was over, the man was obviously delivered. He was shouting with the joy of it.

Fred's eyes were about to roll out on the floor, but I purposely didn't say anything. I didn't want to auto-suggest anything. I said, "What happened to you?"

He said, "Didn't you see it?"

"Didn't I see what?" I let him tell it from the start.

He said, "When we were praying, I opened my eyes, and I saw a big black furry thing come down out of that man's pants' leg, go across his shoe, halfway across the floor, and disappear down the crack. I saw it with my own eyes!"

The man has never doubted the reality of Satan since then. God has answered my prayer. Fred had seen a demon.

Now did it possess the brother, or was it in control, or what? I couldn't care less. He got rid of it. That's better than arguing theology. Praise God that He can bless us beyond our poor ability to figure it all out. The power of the enemy is real, but the power of the living God is more powerful still. And King's kids have ready access to it.

Is this spooky? It might sound like it. To me, as a scientist, it sounds like the most logical, wonderful, sensible arrangement that God could set up. Get on His team and go and be the answer to the world's problems.

Young people want reality today. This is reality. This is where it's at. This is it. This is the power to change lives, the power to live victoriously. This is high-powered King's kid activity. That's what it's all about. Heal the sick. Cast out devils. Do the marvelous things that Jesus did and greater things because He went to the Father. The normal Christian life has to do with acting supernormal. The reason we think it's beyond the normal is because we're so accustomed to dreary, drab, lukewarm Christians that make God sick to His stomach.

The normal Christian life is summed up in the last few verses of the Gospel of Mark in the words of Jesus. He said, "Go ye into all the world, bear fruit. Preach the Gospel to every creature. He that believeth and is baptized shall be saved. But he that believeth not shall be damned. And these signs shall follow them that believe."

197

The first sign is: "In my name shall they cast out devils."
Satan, get out and stay out.

"They will speak with new tongues—" Get on the hot line
to heaven and stay there. Begin to praise God all the time.
"Take up serpents, drink any deadly thing. No harm. Lay
hands on the sick and they shall recover."

After the Lord had spoken to the disciples, He was received up into heaven and sat on the right hand of God, and
they went forth and preached everywhere, the Lord working
with them and confirming the word with signs following.
That's clear-cut directive, isn't it? Act like it. Be a twenti-
eth-century King's kid. The King hasn't changed His instructions or His nature.

28
How to Forgive

Often I say, "Lord, show Your adequacy for this occasion; show Yourself able to handle this mess. Lord, this looks awful to me, and if I had to judge by appearances, I'd give up right now. But I'm judging by Your Word that You are working within me, both to will and to do Your good pleasure." And when I give it all to Him, He furnishes the power to make the new life work out through me to minister life in every situation.

Why doesn't it happen more frequently? Why are Christians less than victorious? There are reasons, hindrances to our receiving all that God has for us. I call these hindrances roadblocks.

God has showed me three basic roadblocks to the pouring out of His power—unforgiveness, impatience, and unbelief. These roadblocks can operate to stop God's power in the life of a minister or in those to whom he wants to minister.

Not long after I began to believe, and after I had received the Baptism in the Holy Spirit, I was complaining because

God wasn't using my ministry in a more powerful way. When I asked Him to show me what the trouble was, He showed me the passage in Matthew where Jesus said that if you bring your gift to the altar and remember that your brother has something against you, you have to leave your gift and go and be reconciled to the brother before you can give your gift to God.

I knew there was a broken relationship that had to be taken care of in my life. And that mess I had made was fogging my signals, fouling up my receiving apparatus. I couldn't hear what God was saying, because I was broadcasting so much static of my own.

One morning, in a drunken stupor—before I was saved—I had gotten out of bed in terrible shape—as usual—and I saw a doctor bill lying on my dresser. It was bad timing. My wife should not have put it there. But I opened it, and I resented it. I got on the phone and told the doctor how many shysters I thought he was, and I said a lot of other things, none of which were complimentary to him or his profession. I really told him off, finishing with, "If you live to be a thousand years old and me ten thousand, I'm never going to pay you that bill—" And I slammed down the phone, burning my bridges behind me.

Time went on. I got saved. Met Jesus. Began to walk this life in the Spirit.

The doctor lived only five or six houses away on a one-way street. I couldn't go anywhere without passing his house. Across the street was a vacant lot, and I'd turn my head and look at the weedy vacant lot. I actually got a northbound crick in my neck from looking that way every time. I didn't want to see the doctor if he happened to be outside, because he bugged me. I didn't want to face the fact that I had behaved like a real pagan with him. I had brought this thing on myself, but I tried to rationalize.

When the Lord showed me the Scripture, I said, "Well, Lord, that's a misprint. He ought to come to me. I'm the injured one. Besides, that's all in the past, water over the dam. Won't do any good to reopen the discussion." But no matter how much I rationalized, God didn't change the Scripture to conform to my way of thinking, and I got more and more miserable.

One night, I was so heavy with guilt, all I could think of was that doctor's name. God brought him to my attention every time I tried to pray. I was dying on the vine spiritually. When you bring your gifts to the altar, when you come in the attitude of prayer and worship, the first name that comes into your head of somebody who bugs you, is your uppermost problem, blocking the kingdom of heaven from coming into evidence in your own life. Awareness of a roadblock brings responsibility to do something about it.

And so one night I was so heavy with guilt, I said, "All right, Lord, I'll go. By Your grace, I'm going to his house and make it right." And I walked past those five houses, like fifty miles. It was too short a run to drive it; I had to walk up, and I knew all the neighbors were looking at me, saying, "There goes the guilty one."

I was so conscious of this guilt that I was sure that everybody was whispering, "There goes the sinner. He's going up and confess."

And Satan was throwing everything in the book at me. "You don't want to go and apologize to him. You don't have to."

"Of course, I don't have to," I agreed with him. "I can die and not apologize. I have a choice of drying up. I have a choice of no answered prayer. Oh, I've got a lot of choices, but they're second, and third, and fourth hand. They're not the best ones. King's kids want first best. And God wants me to have first best, but I'll not get it except God's way."

I knocked on the door, no answer. I heaved a big sigh of relief and slunk back home. It took me several weeks to muster up enough courage and scrape up enough grace to go back the second time. This time his wife answered the door and said, "The doctor's not at home."

The third time, on the way up the walk, I prayed, "Lord, I'm going, but You're going to have to do the doing."

I knocked on his door again. And when he opened the door that day, I shivered. He was several inches taller than I am, and he looked down on me as if I was an annoying worm. He was younger than I am, faster on his feet. And I expected a poke in the nose.

"Lord," I said under my breath, "I don't have anything to say to this man. Give me Your word of wisdom."

The man looked down on me and said, "What do you want?" just like I knew he'd say.

"Doc," I said, "I'd like to come in and talk to you."

"I don't have anything to say to you," he said, and he started to close the door. I stuck my foot in the crack like a rug salesman. I had to get into that man's home— And then the Lord put words in my mouth.

"Doc," I said, "I'm not the kind of person who would be here to ask apologies of you or anyone else, but this is a matter between God and myself, and we'd both appreciate it if you'd let me in." He almost fell over, and I almost fell in.

Those were not my words. That was a word of wisdom direct from heaven, the only words that could have gotten me into that house. We had a good talk, I paid the bill, and confessed to him how I'd been all tangled up with alcohol, in a stupor, and I'd said a lot of unkind things. I wasn't sure just what. But I was there because I had become a Christian—I had met Jesus. I was in a new lifestyle that had to do with getting rid of the muck and garbage of my own making in the past, mending broken relationships and all that. These happened to be two steps in our Alcoholics Anonymous program.

And he said, "Well, I suspected you were having trouble with your drinking, and if we doctors listened to everything that people told us, we'd have to quit or go into an insane asylum." Then he looked straight at me, but not fierce, this time, and said, "As far as forgiveness is concerned, it's all forgotten about." Then we shook hands.

When I went out of the doctor's house, I was right with God because I was right with people. My prayer life, my spiritual life, shot up. It had been closed, shut down, until I went and became reconciled.

But I had to learn the lesson of forgiveness more than once. God will keep putting us through lesson after lesson until we finally learn what we have to know to function with full-time efficiency as King's kids.

About fourteen years ago, God sent me to the conference of an important lay renewal organization in eastern Pennsylvania to introduce to them the Baptism of Jesus, the Baptism in the Holy Spirit. The conferees were mostly denominational people who had never heard of such a thing, just as I never had when I first joined the Baptist church.

Over the years, many hundreds had met Jesus as Baptizer in some of our midnight sessions. But then the Sanhedrin, the hierarchy, caught up with me.

I think it was in the seventh year of my participation when they ordered me to attend no more meetings except the ones announced by the Sanhedrin. I voiced my objections like a devout pagan, and then I went home and pouted under my gourd vine. I said, "Lord, send down the fire of heaven and burn up the whole cotton-picking outfit." Oh, did I throw a pity party! I burned. I sent them a letter which would have done justice to any devil's camp. A few mornings later, the Lord seemed to say, *They really hurt your feelings, didn't they?*

I said, "Lord, they sure did." I thought He was going to encourage me to throw a bigger pity party. But He didn't. Instead it seemed as if the Lord was saying, *They really treated you badly, didn't they?*

And I said, "Lord, You don't know."

Well, He said, *I do—they treated Me that way. Should the servant expect better treatment than the Master?*

I was a little bit ashamed by then, and I said, "No. No, Lord."

It seemed as if He said, *Have you been beaten and left for dead?*

"No."

Have you been shipwrecked?

"No."

Have you been sawn asunder?

"No, Lord, it just felt that way."

Been cast into prison?

All the things that had happened to Paul started to run through my mind. And not one of them had happened to me. And the Lord seemed to say, *Are you serving them or Me?*

"You, Lord."

Well, then, go on back and get thrown out some more.

The second time, it didn't hurt so much. Then He let me off the hook for a couple of years. But about a year ago, I had a feeling I had to go back, because I was still hurting. A hurt has to be corrected where it took place. The sore spot against my Christian brethren was a blockage in my spiritual growth. It had to go. I couldn't correct it just by praying for them. I had to go back to the source.

This is basic in all of life. We have to make amends for past wrongs right where they took place. In Revelation 2:5, the Spirit says, "Go back to where you blew it, and start over." When we stand praying at the altar, and we think of someone who has aught against us, we have to leave our gift at the altar, go make it right, and then come back and offer our gift, our sacrifice. Chances are, we'll be healed on the way back, because that's when healing takes place, when we go and make it right.

I knew I had to go back, but I didn't want to. So I put out a fleece. "Well, Lord, I'll go back *if* they send me a personal written invitation to be on a team." Now, I knew that couldn't happen, because I was on their scratch list.

But somebody goofed—and I received an invitation to be on the team.

I hadn't wanted the Lord to honor my fleece. Now I had to go back. There was no getting out of it. And I don't like getting thrown out of a Christian community in the presence of five or six hundred of the brethren. It hurts my pride when they don't appreciate me anymore. But my likes and dislikes had to be trampled under foot. Victory has to take place at the point where the trouble set in.

And so I drove up to the mountain resort conference on a Friday afternoon. They had a preregistration of about eight hundred, and so they had made plans for about six hundred, anticipating the usual rate of cancellations. But the weather was so beautiful that just about everybody came, including me.

When I arrived at the registration area, the fellow in charge looked through the reservations, said, "Well, I'm sorry, but your name is not on the list." I figured somebody had found out they'd goofed, and so they'd taken my name off the list for a room.

"Well, praise the Lord," I said out loud.

He said, "What did you say?" He was kind of new at this thing, and when I'd repeated myself, he thought he'd got the message. He said, "Yes, praise the Lord for nothing."

"No," I said, "praise Him for the invisible room. God's going to produce a room if He wants me here." I stepped over to one side to wait and see what the Lord was going to do. And I kept on telling Him how it looked to me.

"Now I'll be very delighted to leave, Lord, unless You make provisions for me." This would let me off the hook in good shape, I thought. And I kind of hoped there wouldn't be any room.

This is releasing, again. What we loose on the earth is loosed in heaven. "Lord, it doesn't make any difference to me. If I had my druthers, I'd rather not be here. But that's all right. Do what You want to. I'll just wait."

And so I waited, praising the Lord right there in the midst of all the angry confusion in the so-called registration area. There were six rows of Christians crying to get rooms. There weren't enough rooms even for ones whose names were on the list. I listened to them, and they sounded just like pagans, griping, grumbling, complaining, gossiping, indignant, explosive.

"I came six hundred miles, and they have no room for me—"

"They can't do that to me—"

"I'll fix them—"

Pagan talk.

I kept standing in the middle of all that confusion, saying, "Thank You, Jesus. Praise You, Lord. I don't know where my room is, but You do. I don't need the bed now. It would be in my way. I'd fall over it at three o'clock in the afternoon. I'll need it later on tonight, but right now I don't. But I would like to have my room, because I'd like to move in and clean up. And I'm going to stand here and praise You till something happens. Either they throw me out, or I have a room. It doesn't really matter which. Your will, Lord."

You know how long it took? I timed it—twenty minutes. I stood right there in the middle of that milling throng of pagan-sounding Christians, and I didn't hear one word of praise except out of me. They all looked at me as if I had three heads. They circled me; they gave me a wide berth. And these were born-again brethren! But they were doing their thing in a commonsense way, while I was doing God's thing in a spiritual way. All I was doing was praising— "Thank You, Jesus. Hallelujah! Glory to God! I'm a King's kid."

While I stood there, a woman worked her way through the crowd, with an envelope in her hand. She came right up to me, like a homing pigeon. I didn't know her. She didn't know me. But she held out the envelope toward me and asked, "Could you use my reservation?"

I said, "Aren't you going to use it?"

She shook her head, "My husband just called and said he

can't be here. We had reserved a double room, but I'm going to bunk in with a girl friend. Here's a double room reservation if you can use it."

Well, hallelujah! Glory to Jesus! I had asked the Lord for a single room. He gave me a double because He knew that at midnight that night there were going to be twenty-three people packed into that room to receive the Baptism in the Holy Spirit. That was Friday night.

Saturday night, the group said, "Well, could we have another meeting tonight?"

"Well, of course," I told them. "I'm always ready to brag on Jesus."

So we prepared to move into the TV room in the Inn. It'll seat a hundred and fifty or so. When I was on the way there about midnight, a couple of the members of the Sanhedrin said, "Are you planning to hold one of those meetings tonight?"

I said no, and I was being perfectly honest with them. I don't plan to hold any meetings at all. But sometimes the Lord sets them up and asks me to be there.

Well, they were still a little bit suspicious, and so they asked me another question. "Are you going to attend one?"

I said, "Yes, I'm on my way now."

"Didn't we tell you not to do it anymore?"

I agreed, "You certainly did. You told me that very thing."
One of the Sanhedrin members faked a smile, as if she was going to try the power of positive thinking on me.

"Well, you're not going to, then, are you?"

Her smile fell off fast when I said, "Of course, I am. Any-

time that anyone asks me to share my experience with
Jesus, that's where you're going to find me. Why don't you
come along?"

She said, "Well, you come up here every year and leave a
bunch of emotional wrecks for us to clean up."

And I said, "Sister, why don't you come and find out how
we make emotional wrecks?"

"Oh no, I couldn't do that."

This sister is Spirit-filled. She and her husband, a local
pastor up there, have both received the Baptism and have
been muzzled by the Sanhedrin. They're denying the power.
But that's their problem—and God's—not mine. Mine is to
rejoice, to serve Jesus, and not any Sanhedrin anywhere.

So about a hundred and fifty gathered, and I guess there
were a hundred who received what they came for, because
Jesus always obliges. When you come to the fountain, He
always waters the sheep. Hallelujah!

The next morning at breakfast in the big dining hall, the
Sanhedrin sent a committee of one to ask me to please leave.
But it was too late; the damage was done. Hallelujah! And
the Lord had His victory. There was no more bitterness in
me.

"I'm ready, Lord. You've done Your work here. Let's move
on."

As I started down the woods to my cottage to pack my
bags and leave, I saw two of the sisters, still bubbling, still
praising God in all kinds of languages, walking up the path.
As I approached them, the Spirit of the Lord said, *I will give
you the heathen for your inheritance.*

"Hallelujah! Praise God. I don't *need* any more, but Lord, bring it on." King's kids are glory gluttons—always *ready* for more. And God's always got more for His young'uns. Praise God!

And so I stopped, and the three of us rejoiced. Then one of these two sisters who had received the Baptism the night before—they hadn't even gone to bed—pointed down the path and said, "There comes my roommate, a Hindu woman from India."

The Lord said, *There is the heathen.*

We talked to her a little bit, and it turned out that she had never known that God had a first name, Jesus. She was delighted to hear that you could know God by His first name.

When I left a few minutes later, the glory of heaven was all over her face, and she was praising Jesus.

The heathen for your inheritance. God's always true to His word.

With God, it's always action and more action where King's kids are willing to let God use them to bring forth the impossible. It makes life exciting adventure—no boredom. "Rejoice evermore. Pray without ceasing. In every thing give thanks: for this is the will of God in Christ Jesus for you."

Let us bring unto God continually the sacrifice of praise. That is the fruit of our lips. When you don't feel the least bit like it, say, "Lord, I praise You. I thank You, Jesus, for only one reason—because You said to." Don't ever stop thanking Him. Don't ever stop praising Him.

What if you get thrown out? Go on back and get thrown out some more. Jesus said, *If you're on My team, you'll never win a popularity contest, but the rewards are going to be well worth it.* Turn to Him that day to hear Him say, *Well done, good and faithful servant—not accomplished servant, not wise servant, not big-shot servant, but faithful servant. You've been faithful in a few things—you've dared to praise Me in the face of adversity. Now you're conditioned, now you're trained, so I can put you in charge of a few more things or maybe many things.* It all has to do with our being trained to walk by faith.

How long do you have to study a lesson? Until you learn it. How long will you have a particular problem? Until it is no longer a problem. And then when it goes away, you'll miss it because it has been a real friend. How long must you have your unpleasant mother-in-law on your hands? Only as long as you need her. When you no longer need her ministry, she'll go away—and then you'll invite her back. Praise the Lord!

We need one another in the state we're in. And when we've learned to rejoice evermore, pray without ceasing, in every thing give thanks, then our sights are raised to see what God has in mind for His kids. We have to look above the ordinary, average way of seeing things, and to let His mind begin to function in our think tank, to see things from God's standpoint. In every situation, we have to say, "Lord, what's in it for You?" not, "What's in it for me?

"What's in it for You, Lord? I know there's glory in it for

You, deliverance for me, and blessings for Your young'uns."

Let's go. Let's walk in and possess the land. Inherit the Kingdom prepared for you. Live like a King's kid. In the here and now.

For a free copy of
LOGOS JOURNAL
send your name and address to
Logos Journal
Box 191
Plainfield, New Jersey 07060
and say, "one free Journal, please."